5

WORLD OF CULTURE

COSTUME

by Rachel H. Kemper

Newsweek Books, New York

NEWSWEEK BOOKS

Alvin Garfin, Editor and Publisher

Kathleen Berger, Managing Editor
Edwin D. Bayrd, Jr., Contributing Editor
Mary Ann Joulwan, Art Director
Laurie Platt Winfrey, Picture Editor

Title page: A Sung Dynasty scroll painting, attributed to Emperor Hui Tsung, depicts court ladies ironing a bolt of newly woven silk.

Grateful acknowledgment is made for the use of excerpted material on pages 154–81 from the following works:
After the Banquet by Yukio Mishima. Copyright © 1963 by Alfred A. Knopf, Inc. Reprinted by permission of Alfred A. Knopf, Inc. Translated by Donald Keene.
From *Babbitt* by Sinclair Lewis, copyright, 1922, by Harcourt Brace Jovanovich, Inc.; renewed, 1950, by Sinclair Lewis. Reprinted by permission of the publishers.
Death in Venice and Seven Other Stories by Thomas Mann. Copyright © 1930 and renewed 1958 by Alfred A. Knopf, Inc. Reprinted by permission of Alfred A. Knopf, Inc. Translated by H.T. Lowe-Porter.
The Great Gatsby by F. Scott Fitzgerald. Copyright © 1925 by Charles Scribner's Sons. Reprinted with the permission of Charles Scribner's Sons.

ISBN: Regular edition 0-88225-137-6 ISBN: Deluxe edition 0-88225-138-4
Library of Congress Catalog Card No. 77-78799
© 1977 Europa Verlag. All rights reserved.
Printed and bound by Mondadori, Verona, Italy.

Contents

1

The Invention of Modesty

And the eyes of them both were opened, and they knew that they were naked; and they sewed fig leaves together and made themselves garments.
                                                                    Genesis 3:7

And he said, I heard thy voice in the garden, and I was afraid, because I was naked; and I hid myself.   *Genesis 3:10*

LIKE ADAM, PRIMITIVE MAN was afraid. Indeed his entire, all-too-short existence must have been spent in a miasma of fear. Fear crowded him on every side; fear of starvation, fear of sterility among his women, fear of the elemental forces of nature, fear of sudden death under the rending claws and fangs of more efficiently designed predators. His options were brutally simple: master the fear or descend again into the beasthood from which he so recently had arisen.

Man's first embellishments and rudimentary clothing served as potent weapons in the fight against fear. The use of body paint was the first step in the development of clothing. Its function was entirely magical. Through its power, primitive man attempted to control and modify the forces, natural and supernatural, that dominated his life. Yellow ochre smeared across his body helped him borrow the life-giving power of the sun; white clay or ash paste on his face gave him the grinning countenance of a skull to terrify his enemies; powdered red ochre sifted on the bodies of his dead gave their pallid flesh the semblance of life and enabled their spirits to live again in a better world.

Next came the use of ornament. Necklaces of lions' claws or bears' teeth, assorted amulets of horn, ivory, or bone, capes of leopard or ocelot skin helped early man capture the strength, stealth, and virility both of the animals he preyed upon and those that preyed upon him. Decked out in borrowed finery, man felt an increase of confidence—as he has continued to feel ever since. The lion-skin cloak still retained the animistic power of its original owner, and it also served as a constant and comforting reminder of how its new owner had come to obtain it. The old truism "Clothes make the man" was never more true than here at the dawn of human evolution. Throughout mankind's long infancy, costume was one of the more visible characteristics that distinguished our ancestors from the beasts with whom they shared the plains throughout the endless African summer.

There were several reasons why primitive men chose to clothe their nakedness, but modesty was not one of them. The notion that nudity is shameful—the concept behind the Michelangelo fresco detail opposite—is a fairly recent development in the long history of clothing, and it is one that had no influence on the prehistoric Adams and Eves who were the true inventors of costume. Indeed, it seems likely that men and women alike first covered their genitals to emphasize rather than to hide them.

7

Costume was also used to enhance man's earliest religious rituals. A painting from the cave of Les Trois Frères in southern France, dating to about 20,000 B.C., shows a mysterious figure wearing the antlers and mask of a deer and the skin of some other animal with a long, bushy tail, perhaps a horse or a wolf. The figure, popularly called "The Sorcerer," seems to be dancing. He is heavily bearded and displays his genitals.

Religious costume retained its magical significance throughout much of human history. Approaching a god is a serious business and usually requires special garments. In Western culture, the magical power of religious vestments has declined into mere symbolism. In other civilizations the supernatural value has been carried to extremes, with the Aztecs of ancient Mexico pursuing their belief in the magic of clothing to a logical and grisly conclusion. One of their major deities was Xipe Totec, "Our Lord the Flayed One," "the Drinker by Night," a nature god whose power was expressed in the fertile spring rain. Victims dedicated to him were shot with arrows and then skinned. His priests donned these human skins for special rites at the beginning of the rainy season. Many works of art from that beautiful and doomed culture graphically illustrate this practice. The raw skin was carefully pulled on over the priest's own body, rather like a suit of long underwear, and laced neatly up the back. The feet were removed but the hands were usually retained to dangle horribly at the priest's wrists. The victim's face was also flayed and tied on over that of the priest. This magical act then induced the earth itself to put on a new skin: vegetation that had died during the dry season was born again.

Preoccupation with sex, with female fecundity and male virility, no doubt led to the development of the official fig leaf. Genitals were almost certainly first covered as a form of sexual display rather than from shame. To early man, genitals were sacred, not shameful; the source of life itself rather than the seat of original sin. The crotch came to be covered to protect this life source from evil magic. Modesty, to paraphrase a modern sex goddess, had nothing to do with it. Cowrie shells, shaped like the vulva, were strung together to enhance and protect the female reproductive parts. Leaves, ferns, animal hair, and feathers, selected on the basis of presumed magical potency, were pressed into service.

No doubt these ornaments also called male attention to the sexual availability of the ladies in question. One of the earliest preserved records of female costume supports this theory. A little Paleolithic fertility figure, the Venus of Lespugue, is entirely naked except for a curious apron at the rear, worn under rather than over her buttocks. It is impossible to identify the material, possibly hanks of hair or leather. The strips are fastened to a cord that passes under the monumental backside to lose itself in the heavy thighs and abdomen.

Women were probably the first to cover their sexual organs. It was certainly obvious that this was where children came from although there must have been a great deal of lively conjecture as to what put them there. Eventually, the concept of fatherhood was grasped and, inspired by animistic magic, male sexual display achieved astonishing dimensions. In a hostile environment, survival of the small tribal group

To survive in a hostile world primitive man needed to procreate, and vestigial draperies such as the one that encircles the buttocks of the Venus of Lespugue (above) evolved specifically to enhance their wearer's sex appeal. Fertility rituals were also designed to increase reproduction. In these it was often the males—adorned with skins, antlers, and body paint (right, above)—who were the focus of attention. Fertility—not of humans but of the soil—was the chief concern of agrarian societies such as the Aztec. At right, below, a priest adorned in flayed-out human skin worships the god of spring rains.

depended often on sheer brute force, and male strength and leadership came to be identified with sexual virility.

The first male genital covers must have mimicked a permanent erection and possibly originated when some aging chief, fearful of being deposed, stuffed his drooping parts into a penis sheath that would have staggered Zeus himself. This garment survived among the ancient Libyans well up into historic times. Tribute bearers are shown in Egyptian tomb paintings wearing this characteristic attire, an exaggeratedly long tubular case, supported by a draped baldric and tastefully ornamented with beads and tassels, swinging in the general vicinity of the wearer's knees. The message was plain: no evil spirit would dare to assault such an imposing bastion of strength and virility. The magical power of life rises against the threat of debility and death.

This, then, was where it all began. Paint, ornament, and rudimentary clothing were first employed to attract good animistic powers and to ward off evil. Costume originated in the service of magic and although this motive no longer survives among us on a conscious level, it might be argued that in our subconscious it still reigns supreme.

Once magic formed a precedent for man to hang strange odds and ends around his body, other reasons for wearing costume emerged and remain very much with us. The noted fashion authority James Laver has described these motives as the utility principle, the seduction principle, and the hierarchical principle. Then, as now, men and women were preoccupied with protection, comfort, sexual attraction, and social status.

It used to be assumed that clothing originated as protection against weather, yet millennia must have passed before man migrated to a climate where that consideration arose. Once man began to think in terms of comfort, his ingenuity was given full rein in devising garments to keep out the weather—arctic snow, torrential rains, or tropical sun. By and large, such costumes have been designed strictly for utility and have had a minimal effect on the development of fashion.

Protective clothing for warfare, for dangerous activity, or for strenuous sports tells another story altogether. Status comes into this as well as mere utility. A garment to keep off the rain, no matter how elegantly designed, lacks glamour. Garments intended to deflect the point of a lance, flying arrows, or solar radiation possess a strange kind of instant chic and are sure to be modified into fashions for both men and women. Contemporary examples abound: the ubiquitous aviator glasses that line the rails of fashionable singles bars, perforated racing gloves that grip the wheels of sedate family cars, impressively complicated scuba divers' watches that will never be immersed in any body of water more challenging than the country-club pool.

This curious fashion trend has been around ever since the Renaissance when the dukes of Berri and Brittany, indolent and pampered, had cuirasses stitched of white satin in imitation of plate mail. There are other examples from that period. Armor was designed, in the mid-sixteen century, with what was called a "peasecod belly," a sharply pointed projection of the torso which produced a rather grotesque pigeon-breasted effect. The design was eminently practical; it provided a smooth, curved surface with no fussy ornament or concave areas that would catch the point of a lance. The tip of an opponent's weapon would slide off harmlessly.

But stripped of his armor by a squire and dressed for dinner, the man of fashion retained the same peculiar shape. His doublet was heavily whaleboned and padded, causing it to stand away from the natural lines of the body. His trunk hose, or slops, were also boned to imitate the steel skirts of the armor. The same basic lines carried over into the bodices of women's fashions, although the peasecod effect was minimized and the torso was flatter, with nature fully constrained under marvelous contraptions of bone, wood, and steel. The implication, for the gentlemen, was that they were already dressed as if in armor and immediately prepared to cover themselves with glory on the field of honor. What the ladies were expected to cover themselves with is equally obvious but less blatantly expressed; certainly they would have had to be pried out of those corsets first.

An interesting aspect of sports costume is its curious lack of consistency. The ancient Greeks exercised and competed stark naked, a custom which perhaps accounts for their ban on female spectators at the games. Their sole gesture toward protection was the practice of binding the genitals with a soft cord so as to tuck them up in the groin out of harm's way. Even so, the thought of the all-out, no-holds-barred *pankration* must have given many an aspirant second thoughts.

This inconsistency is still apparent in professional sports. A football player goes helmeted and padded, looking like a cross between King Kong and the Thing from Outer Space. Baseball players, in honor of the ninety-mile-an-hour-plus fastball, are permitted batting helmets and a protective cup familiarly known, according to Jim Bouton, as a "ding-dong." Alas for basketball. Since it is officially designated as a noncontact sport, its players are reduced to a thin uniform, an ordinary supporter, and an apprehensive smile.

In the future it is not entirely impossible that the linebacker's helmet or the goaltender's mask might appear, gussied up, as an element of formal attire. It has happened in the past. A classic and often cited example is the top hat. It was originally designed to be worn on the fox hunt—"the unspeakable in pursuit of the inedible." If the horse stopped suddenly and the rider didn't, the stiff topper would cushion the collision. Within fifty years of its introduction to the English sporting scene, the top hat became an indispensable part of evening attire and is still seen today at fashionable weddings and gangsters' funerals.

The seduction principle has always figured prominently in women's fashions. Throughout the greater part of Western history it has been woman's role, indeed almost her only option, to seduce men into marriage. Fashion functioned as an element of direct or indirect seduction, since during long centuries women could scarcely exist socially or economically on their own and were confined under the protection of their nearest male relative. The degree of a woman's well-being for the greater part of her life, her affluence and social position, depended entirely upon those of the man to whom, quite literally, she was given. Woman's only stock in trade was what was bluntly known as her "commodity." When the merchandise went on the market, it was only

Modesty has long dictated that a woman should conceal her physical attributes; morality has dictated how well. During the reign of pious Philip II of Spain, somber colors, bound bosoms, stiff corsets, and excessive padding (left, above) reflected the asceticism of the age. Two and a half centuries later, fashionable women of the French Directoire (left, below) dressed for a more permissive age in sheer fabrics that revealed rather than constrained the figure. As French fashions changed toward the end of the nineteenth century, muslin gave way to velvet, and white to black. Billowing fabrics, flowers and jewelry, and vast expanses of alabaster skin were à la mode, as the Ingres portrait of Mme Moitessier seen above plainly indicates.

common sense to dress it up as attractively as possible.

Seduction in dress was greatly helped along by the invention of modesty. The concept of modesty probably originated as a sophisticated reaction against the primitive custom of sexual display. Clothes may "resemble a perpetual blush upon the surface of humanity," but by concealing the greater part of the body, they arouse an unholy curiosity to know what's actually under all that yardage. Sexual emphasis in women's fashions changes rapidly. Over a period of a relatively few years in almost any given century since the fourteenth, emphasis will shift from the hips to the belly to the bust and back again. In this century we have enjoyed the added attraction of legs, to say nothing of backbones and belly buttons. Apparently, men get bored with the same scenery and need the constant refreshment of new landscape.

Modesty in clothing, particularly in women's clothing, is usually an excellent indicator of the social and religious standards of any given period. During the early Middle Ages, in a society dominated by the Church, clothing was quite conservative, covering and disguising the figure. Formal costume for men and women was similar, very nearly identical. In cathedral sculptures or in manuscript illuminations, about the only way sex can easily be determined is by checking to see who wears the beard. Normally, the unisex look is to be found only in societies where little emphasis is placed on sex other than for the laudable purpose of procreation. Consider the uniformly trousered masses of modern China. Today's unisex look is another matter entirely. Sex per se is still important, almost obsessively so, but sex-stereotyped roles are increasingly obsolescent.

Extreme modesty in costume usually indicates a repressed or regimented society. Spanish styles of the mid to late sixteenth century provide an excellent example. In this era, manners were formal and morality was rigorous. Society was repressive both politically and intellectually; there was little social mobility or personal freedom and there was even a system of ideological thought control, the Inquisition. Women's costume was severe and angular, the torso totally flattened under heavy corsetry, the sleeves padded to give a geometric, unnatural line to the arm. Strong, tough velvets or heavy satins and damasks were favored; rich, dark colors were preferred.

By contrast, the era of the French Directoire was a period of extreme freedom. Society was mobile, manners were relaxed, morality was considered to be a matter of personal inclination rather than public decree. This state of affairs was reflected directly in women's costume with its strong neoclassic trend. Garments were simple, uncorseted, and as easy as their wearer's virtue. Underwear was normally not worn at all, and dresses were often wrung out in water before putting them on so that they clung more closely and revealingly to the body. A great lady's ball gown might weigh all of five ounces and could be drawn through a ring. The hairstyles were soft and tousled; women had a "just out of bed" appearance, which may very well have been the case. The thinnest, most delicate silks and muslins, inevitably white, were worn. Touches of color were introduced in trimmings and accessories, but decoration was held to a minimum.

The quality of seduction in clothing largely depends on what type of female is considered most sexually desirable at any given time. In the mid-nineteenth century, polite society was dominated by mature matrons who had passed their first youth and, if truth be told, were quite well along in their second. Their gowns emphasized a vast expanse of creamy bosom, elegant bare arms, a tiny waist, and massive haunches. Majestic, well-fleshed, sophisticated, slightly world-weary, they gaze out of the canvases of Ingres with a placid and somewhat bovine air.

Youthful innocence also had its charms. Billows of white muslin provided a pleasant alternative to the flowing yards of heavy velvets. Afternoon gowns of roughly the same period, tiered and flounced with ruffles, were set off with only the most delicate embroidery or narrow black ribbons. The effect was naïve, childlike, and wickedly alluring. On young women, such costumes must have been irresistible. Older women would have done well to avoid them lest, in the words of the time, they resemble "mutton done up like lamb."

Matron or child, both costumes indicate the generally subservient role of women in a basically male society. Throughout most of Western civilization, women's clothing has been designed deliberately to inhibit or prevent free movement, to limit action, and hence to limit freedom. Hoop skirts, hobble skirts, corsets, and high heels all have been highly touted in the name of fashion and all have been physically restrictive. Wearing the pants—or the shorts, or the kilt—men have generally been free to carry on an active life. Women, by contrast, have been kept in skirts and, until the present century, the skirts were long and voluminous. Nothing could speak louder of the male determination to keep women barefoot and pregnant. Only in the present century with the increasing independence and liberation of women has the basic stereotype—and the basic costume—altered appreciably.

Traditionally, women have dressed for seduction, men have dressed for status. Consider, briefly, how impossible social relations would become if everyone went naked. In a restaurant you would not be able to tell the waiter from the customers. A policeman would look the same as a burglar. A lawyer or judge would be indistinguishable from the prisoner at the bar; there's often little enough difference as it is.

Throughout history, Western and non-Western, lack of clothing has normally indicated a lack of status. In ancient Egypt, children went happily naked until they reached puberty. They had no status, loved and cherished though they were. Slaves were unclothed; they were nonpersons. In pre-Inca Peru, the Mochica immediately stripped their prisoners of war, removing their emblems of rank and their humanity.

The modern world does not strip, it merely humiliates. An elegantly turned-out prostitute, thrown in the slammer, is issued black oxfords with Cuban heels, ankle socks, plain cotton dresses, and underwear with bras laundered flat and useless. In 1944, at the trial of the generals who had conspired against Hitler, the defendants were outfitted in old, nondescript clothes, deprived of collars, neckties, and suspenders. A once-proud field marshal, even his false teeth gone, could only mumble in the dock, fumbling at his beltless trousers like a dirty old man.

The military mind has always been particularly obsessed with

In every society, from the most aboriginal to the most advanced, clothes are the first and foremost index of status. They identify the priesthood, the military, the merchant class—and in so doing automatically reinforce the notions of caste and rank. There is, for example, no mistaking the power and pelf of the Mayan princes seen at lower right; their "borrowed finery"—jaguar skins, quetzal plumes, jade, and shells —bespeaks their privileged place in Mesoamerican society. The same was true of the samurai of feudal Japan. Their heavily embellished armor, generally surmounted by a lacquered steel mask (right, above), set them apart from the rest of Japanese society as completely as did their professional code of ethics.

status: "You salute the uniform and not the man." In warfare it is obviously necessary to have costume coded in such a way that rank can be immediately determined and friend can be distinguished from foe. Even the drab and khaki-clad armies of today retain this system of identification, although the sartorial splendors of a military levee at the Court of St. James's are long gone. In the days of the Napoleonic Wars, the presence chamber was a mass of color; naval officers in blue and gold, infantry in scarlet, light infantry in a multitude of colors, foreign allies in greens, blues and white, the glitter of stars and decorations, the somber richness of fur, the swirling robes of the Knights of the Garter, of the Bath and of St. Patrick, topped off with bearskins, plumed helmets, cockaded top hats, bicornes, and tricornes.

Such magnificence is by no means restricted to the Western world. The armor of the Japanese samurai reveals a similar pride in military arts and an equal obsession with rank. His armor was built out in a series of flaps or plates of lacquered metal that gave him an impressive bulk. A steel mask, modeled into a permanent snarl, protected his face. Ancient Americans wore less armor, but they dressed in gorgeous costumes to indicate their status. The Mayan frescoes from Bonampak in southern Mexico show splendidly appareled warriors and chieftains

wearing fiber headdresses with animal and marine motifs backed by huge sweeps of iridescent quetzal feathers; jaguar skins held in place by richly embroidered belts; ankles, wrists, and chests loaded with jewelry made from shells, gold, and jade. They were, in actual fact, dressed to kill.

In civilian life, too, men have habitually dressed to indicate their position in the pecking order. In the past, clothing was often regulated by sumptuary laws, which precisely defined who was permitted to wear what. More often, the unwritten but equally rigid laws of society determined these customs. An eighteenth-century sprig of the nobility, for example, would have sent his lackeys to beat the presumptuous middle-class counterjumper who had the temerity to wear a sword.

The pursuit of status is the driving force behind fashion. As William Hazlitt remarked, "Fashion is gentility running away from vulgarity and afraid of being overtaken." But what the human race has come up with in the way of clothing to proclaim status pales before the ingenuity exercised, at one time or another, to customize the human body. The morbid pastime of cutting, painting, constricting, and otherwise improving on basic anatomy is probably rooted in protective magic. The still-common practice of circumcision, for all the medical tootle about health and hygiene, would seem to confirm this. In Egypt, parts of Africa and the Americas, heads of infants were bound to produce an elegantly sloping cranium. Mayan infants had a bead tied to a strand of hair hanging down over their nose to ensure a fashionable cross-eyed glare when they grew up. Constrictive leg bandages were used in the Caribbean and arm rings in Melanesia, forcing the muscles to bulge mightily on either side. Tattooing has been widely practiced in all parts of the globe; a full tattoo suit can still be seen, though rarely, in downtown Tokyo. Body scarification, though less common, can still be found in Africa, particularly among Dahomean ladies of rank who allow themselves to be carved like a Christmas goose for purely cosmetic purposes. Men and women have worn ear spools so enormous that an arm could be inserted through the distorted lobe; nose ornaments that pierced and distorted the septum were once popular; front teeth have been filed to elegant points or knocked out altogether to accommodate ornate lip jewels.

As might be expected, women suffered the worst. In provincial African courts at the turn of the century, young girls were force-fattened to hopeless obesity. The wives of the king of Karagwe could not stand up; the explorer John Speke commented of one, "her features were lovely but her body was as round as a ball." In old China, the feet of high-born women were cruelly bound and compressed to form the prestigious Golden Lilies. Her bride price depended directly upon the size of her feet; her tiny shoes were exhibited to the prospective in-laws during the marriage negotiations. From the age of three or four until death, there was no respite from constant, tormenting agony.

That sort of thing can't happen here? On the contrary, the twentieth century provides unparalleled opportunities for improving on nature. It has not been all that long since the great beauty Anna Held had her lower ribs surgically removed to reduce her waist to thirteen inches.

The high price of high fashion is not always measured in terms of dollars; sometimes it is more accurately assessed in terms of human suffering. Foot binding, tattooing, ritual scarification, cosmetic surgery—all cause physical pain, yet all have been endured in fashion's name. Styles differ, but the impulse to reshape the body is constant, whether it is to distend the ear lobes with metal spools (above) or produce a wasp waist by surgically removing the lower ribs (opposite).

Society doctors today could tell of toes amputated to permit a smaller shoe size. Skin can be burned with chemicals to remove freckles or abraded with pumice to discourage wrinkles. Face lifts are common. Noses are pruned right and left. What God has forgotten is no longer simulated with cotton, it is injected with silicone. Breasts can be lifted, rears likewise, and an entire body lift is available for those who can pay the price.

Men are by no means immune to the siren call of instant youth and virility. They can now obtain so-called scalp transplants, in actuality this means a wig sewn to wires embedded in the scalp. They often pull loose. Hair implants are available; in this operation small plugs of hair are simply gouged out and resettled in more barren regions. Compared to the cosmetic surgeons of today, the beauty experts of the ancient world were pikers.

It would be difficult to cite a single human culture wholly innocent of cosmetics. The magical function of body paint faded with the dawn of civilization, but the paint itself remained as ornament. Men and women have decorated their faces and bodies in all the colors of the rainbow. Aztec ladies painted their faces a creamy yellow and dyed their teeth red or black; Japanese geishas preferred a dazzling porcelain-white complexion; Roman and Etruscan warriors favored a coating of red lead for victory celebrations; and the ancient Briton stained himself blue with woad. Conventional face painting has been a standard aspect of fashion from ancient Egypt to the present.

The hair of the head—or of the male face—has been similarly subjected to improvement. Coiffures have been constructed with the aid of such diverse ingredients as clay, tallow, lime, bear grease, and cow manure. The sprays, gels, lotions, and lacquers of today no doubt smell better but the function is the same. Fashion has often dictated hair styles so complex that they were combed out and re-erected on a monthly rather than a daily basis. And the story, possibly apocryphal, is still told in beauty salons across the United States, of the young woman who expired from the bites of spiders that had nested in her overteased, oversprayed, and unwashed bouffant.

There is probably nothing, no matter how painful or repulsive, that will cause humankind to hesitate in the pursuit of beauty; no costume, however uncomfortable or ridiculous, that will not be flaunted with pride in the name of fashion. Fashion functions and has always functioned as a means of wish fulfillment. Throughout the ages, women have wished to appear young, radiantly gorgeous, and infinitely desirable. Men have sought to look virile, distinguished, rich, and superior. In all countries, climes, and eras, both men and women have pursued the elusive goals of status and recognition, attributes which are usually the prerogative of wealth and social position. By following or, better yet, by setting the current fashion, we constantly identify ourselves with the social group, the ideal, of our choice. We are still very much convinced that clothes make the man. Intellectually, perhaps, we know better; emotionally we remain true believers. By providing us with psychological security, fashion becomes not merely a luxury but a necessity. Indeed, if fashion did not already exist, we should have to invent it.

2

Civilizing Costume

FOR UNCOUNTED CENTURIES man stalked the plains of Africa, splendidly tricked out in colorful paint, his body hung with ornaments of bone, teeth, claws, feathers, and shells, his private parts shielded against malignant forces, his shoulders, head, or waist draped with trophy skins attesting to his skill as a hunter. He moved northward across the land bridges that then linked the shores of the Mediterranean, following in the tracks of the great animal herds. As he continued his long trek, he probably became aware of a steadily increasing chill in the air. One morning he awoke to find the ground blanketed with snow. Without intending to, man had just entered the Ice Age.

By then, our ancestors had probably lost most of their body hair. A commonly accepted explanation of the "naked ape" mutation is that a hairless hide permits rapid cooling of the body during and after bursts of strenuous activity, like running down game. The loss of body hair and the increase in the number of sweat glands were prime survival factors in the development of early man. To compensate for the loss of his fur coat, man developed a thick layer of subcutaneous fat. But along the fringes of the ice sheets that covered northern Europe, this natural insulation was not enough. Something new was about to be added.

From then on, animals were tracked down and killed for their pelts as well as for their flesh. A thick bearskin, once the bear had no further use for it, went a long way toward keeping out the cold. But problems arose. For one thing, fresh hides reek to heaven. Although it is not likely that early man felt aesthetic revulsion against the stinking, slimy hides he was forced to wear, the stench would have clogged his keen hunter's nose and unnecessarily have advertised his presence to the game he pursued. Moreover, when hides dry out they become stiff and unmanageable. By way of remedy, it was found that patient, steady mastication of a raw hide renders it soft and pliable. To this day, Eskimo women follow this procedure, literally chewing the fat far into the Arctic night. Oils and fats rubbed into the leather work even better, although, like the chewing, the process has to be repeated if the garment gets wet.

The discovery of tanning must have been accidental. Some ancient genius found an animal hide that had soaked for a long time in a pool with rotting oak or willow bark and discovered that the pelt remained supple and impervious to water. Perhaps it was his wife who figured out how to shape and stitch the hide to fit the body. The earliest true garment was probably similar to a poncho, a hide with a hole cut in it to admit the wearer's head, then lapped and tied around the waist. Although warm and protective, it must also have been cumbersome, flapping about and getting in the way. But cutting and tailoring made the garment more efficient. At first holes were punched with stone or bone awls and the pieces laced together with sinew or hair. Little perforated bone plates were used as stitching guides. The eyed needle, crafted of bone or antler, was invented at least 40,000 years ago.

Paleolithic costume probably evolved into an outfit similar to traditional Eskimo attire—a semifitted jacket and pants. A fully flayed outhide from a large animal, complete with the skin from the fore and hind legs, would automatically have suggested a shape appropriate for men. Interestingly enough, prehistoric women seem to have worn fairly long skirts and shawls, sexual differentiation in clothing thus appearing very early. But there is probably a simple explanation: tailoring pants and jackets out of heavy furs would have been a long, painstaking, and boring task. Women, largely confined to the caves and the care of children, did not need the same kind of physical mobility or protection that men required. A simple wrap-around skirt and loosely draped shawl or poncho would have provided more than enough warmth and taken considerably less trouble to make. Even today, the home sewer who faces the most complicated Vogue Couturier patterns without blinking an eye would think twice before attempting a fully tailored suit for her spouse.

In other, more temperate parts of the world, additional discoveries were being made. At some remote point in time, the people of central Asia discovered felt. Most likely this material was invented by herdsmen who wanted warm clothing but did not want indiscriminately to kill off their domestic animals to get it. To make felt, animal hair is combed out, spread in layers on the ground or on a mat, thoroughly wetted and beaten, stamped, or rolled until the fibers mat together. Apparently it was often given a particularly fine finish by dragging lengths of it across several miles of Siberian steppes at the tail of a galloping horse. Felt is extremely useful. It can be produced in all grades from fine to coarse and used for clothing, blankets, rugs, or tents. It does not drape gracefully, but neither does it ravel. Moreover, it can be cut and tailored with ease into fitted garments. Central Asia has given the world the caftan and the shaped jacket, costumes that still retain the crisp lines of their felt or leather prototypes.

In tropical and subtropical areas, cloth was made from the soft inner bark of certain trees. Strips of bark were peeled from young branches or new shoots, then soaked and beaten as in the felting process, until the fibers adhered together. Since the material does not lend itself to sewing or tailoring, it is usually made up into simple rectangular panels and wrapped around the waist like the traditional Oceanian sarong.

Weaving was invented at a remarkably early date. The origins of the craft are lost in primeval mist, but the plaiting and knotting techniques of the Mesolithic era—for fishing nets, basketry, and the like—

Flocks of domesticated sheep and goats were plentiful in the river valleys of the Near East and fur-bearing animals were scarce. It followed, then, that fabrics should replace pelts as man's identification of status and protection against the elements. The Sumerian statuette at left presents an example of the ubiquitous male garb of the era—a skirt of bulky, fleecy fabric that hung to mid-calf in front and sported a padded tuft in the rear. By the time Gudea (above) ascended the throne of Lagash around 2130 B.C., the tufted kilt had largely been superseded by a plain but substantial woolen cloth draped to cover the left shoulder and arm. The Mesopotamian monarch also wears a lambskin cap with a turned-up brim.

may have provided the inspiration. In any event, weaving was rarely attempted before mankind settled down in permanent agricultural communities. Looms tend to be heavy and nomadic peoples would surely have found them a crushing burden. Even today, wandering pastoral tribes in central Asia do not weave their own cloth, although their economy is based on flocks of sheep and goats. They buy fabric from townsmen; in ages past they would have worn felt or leather. The craft of weaving is unknown to them.

The Neolithic period emerged in recognizable form between 9000 and 8000 B.C. The discoveries of agriculture and stockbreeding enabled our ancestors, with some grumbling no doubt, to forego their nomadic existence and to settle in permanent village communities. The flocks provided wool; flax and cotton were cultivated; the women spun thread and settled down to the serious business of perfecting the world's first major invention, the loom. Although societies have been known where weaving was men's work, normally in the ancient world it was done by women. Almost certainly women were responsible for the basic design of this complicated device. The earliest fabrics were plain tabby weave, the simple over-and-under technique still used by kindergarten children for potholders and place mats. In time, the design of the loom was refined by the addition of bars or sheds that raised or lowered the warp in various combinations to produce patterned weaving. Once weaving became a standard feature of village life, costume as we know it developed rapidly.

Village domesticity was not achieved overnight. Many men must deeply have regretted the lost freedom of the good old days when they hunted by day and swapped lies around the campfire at night. Trotting around after a flock of tame sheep clearly lacks the excitement and prestige of the hunt. Many early farmers and herdsmen were surely reluctant to abandon their skins, the success symbols of former times, and they must have regarded with suspicion the newfangled cloth their womenfolk were weaving and wearing.

The earliest male costume from the ancient Near East was a compromise, combining the authority of fur with the convenience of cloth. The garment, called the kaunakes, was the world's first example of fake fur. It was made by threading tufts of wool or loosely rolled yarn through a coarsely woven cloth panel. The tufts were inserted in neat rows and brushed or combed toward the hem of the garment. The result was a long, shaggy kilt that must have looked a great deal like a flokati rug. In some of the early examples, a large tuft like a tail was retained at the rear. Eventually Sumerian males were eased into plain, heavy woolen cloth with tufts retained only as a decorative fringe.

The basic Sumerian garment was an unsewn rectangular piece of cloth wrapped around the body and fastened on the left shoulder, leaving the right arm free. For greater display of wealth or position, a second garment was added, a shawl that could be draped around the shoulders and worn in any number of ways. The wool was dyed a variety of colors; bright red, saffron yellow, blue, and deep olive green were particularly favored in ancient Mesopotamia. The basic garments themselves were thickly overlaid with fringes, jeweled bands

and borders, rich embroidery, and decorative tassels. The effect was brilliant and sumptuous. On the other hand, nakedness or a mere loincloth was the badge of slavery, although priests—as slaves of the gods—often went naked on ceremonial occasions. By and large, in the Land Between the Two Rivers, costume served to define and enhance social status. Fashions were set by great lords and ladies, who in the pursuit of dignity quietly and stoically perspired into the many layers of their heavy court costumes.

In ancient Egypt clothing developed along other lines entirely. Garments there were woven from cotton and linen; wool was held in contempt as something worn only by barbarians. For priests it was ritually unclean. The Egyptians dressed for comfort, cleanliness, and eventually elegance. The costume of the Old Kingdom (c. 2680–2258 B.C.) was simple and minimal. Pharaoh or slave, men wore loincloths wrapped around the body and fastened in front. They could be wrapped or draped in any number of ways, worn long or short, pleated or unpleated, or starched to a stiff, pyramid-shaped front panel, but for centuries the loincloth remained the basic and almost the only article of male attire. Women wore straight sheath dresses supported by shoulder straps. Sometimes the straps were broad and covered the breasts; sometimes the breasts were left bare. The dresses, normally made of white linen, were often ornamented with embroidery, beads, and what appears to be featherwork. They were made from rectangular pieces of linen sewn up the side. Artistic conventions show them as skintight; in reality they must have been more loosely fitted.

The Egyptians were not clothes conscious; they were body conscious. The attention they did not give to clothing was lavished on their bodies. They bathed frequently, washed their linen daily, and spent

Linen—light, cool, and easy to launder—was the basis of virtually every Egyptian garment from slave's loincloth to pharaoh's haik. Woven (right) from the flax that grew in abundance in the Nile Valley, this naturally white cloth was draped and pleated into hundreds of different shapes. In the fresco detail at left, a god is flanked by female attendants who wear the body-hugging linen sheath that was known as the kalasiris.

hours on personal grooming. Body hair was not tolerated. Both sexes shaved all over with elegant crescent-bladed razors and rubbed their skins with fine pumice. Their heads, too, were usually shaved, then covered with a headcloth or, on gala occasions, elaborate wigs of animal hair or vegetable fiber. Eyebrows were kept in line with delicate tweezers or removed entirely for ritual mourning, as for example, upon the death of the family's sacred cat.

Oils, pastes, lotions, and perfumes were used lavishly; at dinner parties a thoughtful host would provide his guests with cones of perfumed ointment for their heads. These would slowly melt, drenching the wearer's wig in rare scents of myrrh or cinnamon. Cosmetics were essential. Ladies of rank were expected to be their own beauticians, adept at concocting and applying beauty aids. They used foundation creams to lighten their skins and colored their lips and cheeks with an orange-tinted rouge. Fingernails and toenails were painted with a henna stain. Eye make-up was especially important, kohl was used as an eye liner and powdered green malachite as eye shadow.

To offset their white linen, the Egyptians wore jewelry of unparalleled magnificence. Both men and women favored the broad collar, a deep semicircular bib composed of beads strung in many rows and often ornamented in back with a heavy counterweight. Pendants in the form of amulets were worn, rings were popular, and bracelets were often crowded on from wrist to elbow. Precious and semiprecious stones were used, but glass, "the stone that melts," cast in tiny decorative shapes, was also popular. Gold, of course, was preferred above all, for it symbolized the eternal and incorruptible flesh of the sun and was thought to promote eternal survival in the afterlife.

All of these charming earthly treasures were laid away with their owners in the House of Eternity: golden razors and tweezers; brushes, sticks, and tubes for eye make-up; manicure sets, combs and curling irons; mirrors of polished silver supported by naked slave girls; opulent trinkets for the wig; necklaces, crowns, breastplates, collars, bracelets, anklets, rings, girdles, and earrings; and, of course, the cosmetics chest, stuffed with tiny bottles, jars, boxes, phials, and pots. No other ancient civilization communicates so clearly, directly, and intimately with us across the gulf of centuries.

Living under an implacable sun, the ancient Egyptians had little use for elaborate clothing, and their basic costume—the loincloth (right)—remained essentially unchanged for millennia. Another concession to the heat and to their passion for personal cleanliness was the removal of all body hair. Women as well as men wore their hair close-cropped or shaved their skulls entirely, then donned complicated wigs (left) for festive occasions. Other forms of ornamentation and items of personal apparel served largely symbolic functions. In the tomb painting detail below, a pharaoh is identified by his false beard and tenpin shaped crown, a priest by his sacred leopard-skin cape.

Egypt's costume changed very little during the three thousand years of its history. The religion, social structure, and moral philosophy of the country were conservative, based on a deep belief in the eternal stability of the universe. The basic costume was occasionally modified, and a few more garments were introduced from time to time, but no radical changes occurred. In the New Kingdom (*c.* 1786–1314 B.C.) the old straight gown, the kalasiris, became more elaborate. It was now made of almost transparent linen, finely pleated, and wrapped around the body in various ways. Sometimes it was cut with sleeves, sometimes merely draped and tied to give a sleeved bat-wing effect. It might be modestly sewn together or left open in front exposing the body from the waist down. One shoulder, even one breast could be bared, but at this time it was not usual to expose both breasts. The fabric could be treated or draped to cling tightly to the body, delineating each curve.

Gowns acted as a showcase for a beautiful body, calling attention to it in ways that simple nudity could not. In Egyptian art, goddesses are often depicted wearing older styles, while mortals wear newer fashions, but Egyptian costume was basically timeless. The Great Royal Wife of the pyramid builder Khafre could have appeared 2,500 years later at the court of Cleopatra in the dress of her own era and have caused no more stir than a few lifted eyebrows.

Men's costume changed even less. Royalty might go in for longer loincloths, semitransparent kilts with heavy jeweled girdles, or draped gowns similar to those worn by women, but this was about the limit. White was still predominant, but a few pale tints were added—light greens, blues, or yellows, since linen did not take richly colored dyes. Red was seldom used. It was associated with the red-haired, ass-eared Set, the evil brother of the god Osiris, and was considered unlucky.

Royal and priestly costume was consciously symbolic. The pharaoh might wear the simple headcloth, but he also had a battery of crowns for different occasions, the Red Crown of Lower Egypt, the White Crown of Upper Egypt, the Double Crown (a combination of the two), and the Blue Crown, which was adapted from a military helmet. In a uniformly clean-shaven society the pharaoh wore a short, stiff false beard fastened behind his ears. Even the great queen Hatshepsut wore such an article when she ruled Egypt as the female Horus.

Royalty also wore the haik, a large rectangular piece of very thin cloth, knotted and draped around the body so that the wearer appeared to have on three garments—a short kilt, a tunic with flaring sleeves, and a long cloak. It appears only in the New Kingdom, after the Hyksos invasion of the Second Intermediate Period, and may indicate Asiatic influence. Priests wore an elaborate tunic with double skirts and a separate scarf tied around the hips. They also wore a ritual leopard skin draped over the right shoulder. It was the only article from an animal source permitted to them. Even their sandals were made of papyrus.

Some fascinating garments were recovered from the tomb of Tutankhamen. Directly over his shaven skull the young king wore a tightly fitted cap woven of fine linen and embroidered wih the uraeus, the sacred cobra, in tiny gold and blue glass beads. Around his waist,

The ancient Egyptians believed
that all personal ornaments had
beneficient powers, and most of
the amulets they wore served a
ritualistic as well as decorative
purpose. The Eighteenth Dynasty necklace at left, for in-
stance, is dominated by the sacred scarab, a representation of
the sun god, and flanked by two
blue-skinned baboons who greet
the morning sunrise. The corselet above, part of the legendary treasure of the boy-phar-
aoh Tutankhamen, is an intricate composition of gold and
lapis lazuli, turquoise and carnelian, jasper and enamel.

over his funerary wrappings, he wore a ceremonial apron composed of seven gold plates inlaid with multicolored glass and threaded together with bead borders. Chests of clothing had been buried with him.

Among the ruins of Tutankhamen's rotting finery two unusual robes were found in a fair state of preservation. They were long, loose linen garments, decorated along the sides and bottom and around the neck with intricately woven tapestry and fringe. They were made from a rectangular piece of cloth folded in the middle and sewn along the sides with the seams left open near the fold for the arms. A circle was cut for the neckline and a slit was left down the front to ease the garment over the head. The robes look rather like the short dashikis that have enjoyed such popularity in the United States the past few years. Such robes, curiously enough, are not pictured in the art of the times. Apparently they were worn only for special ceremonies.

A pair of tapestry gloves have been found which seem to match the gala robes. They are quite modern in construction, consisting of two pieces of fabric joined, boxlike, by a narrow band of contrasting fabric running along the edge of the hand and between the fingers. The leggings found in the tomb are quite un-Egyptian, more like contemporary après-ski lounging socks, meant to fasten a little below the knee with tapes. The feet have separate pockets for the big toe like the tabi, the traditional sock of Japan. Like the ceremonial robes, such leggings are not shown in Egyptian art. Unable to cope with anything so atypical of the Nile valley, archaeologists originally identified them as archers' gloves. Garments like these lend a cautionary note to the study of Egyptian costume. Egyptian art, the primary source of our information about daily life, was formal and conventionalized, with limited poses and attitudes. Egyptian costume may have been much more inventive and varied than the tomb paintings and sculpture would suggest.

The tomb of Tutankhamen also yielded a splendid corselet, a garment often shown on the monuments but never before recovered in actual form. Small wonder, since it is precisely the sort of thing an enterprising tomb robber would have gone after first. It consisted of a broad panel of tiny gold scales inlaid with carnelian, joined with jeweled straps and an elaborate pectoral amulet to a broad, jeweled collar.

No people before or since have been so stubbornly resistant to the influence of foreign costumes as were the Egyptians. In the New Kingdom, in the Nineteenth and Twentieth dynasties (1320–1085 B.C.), Egypt conquered a great deal of the Near East and held its kingdoms to tribute. Egypt's artists were fascinated by foreign clothing and rendered it in minute detail in tomb paintings showing long lines of tribute bearers coming to prostrate themselves before a Rameses or a Seti. The nations of the Mediterranean are represented time and time again—Nubians, Libyans, Assyrians, Babylonians, Mitanni, Hatti and Hurri, Edomites and Elamites, Minoans and Mycenaeans—all rigged out in a wild variety of robes, tunics, gowns, shawls, loincloths, kilts, and penis sheaths. But only once did a foreign nation directly influence Egyptian style: in the late Eighteenth Dynasty the young bloods at

Although the gilded statuette at left depicts Sekhemet, the lion-headed goddess of war, the deity is garbed in mortal finery. Kala-siris of sheer—sometimes even transparent—linen were worn by all upper-class women. The imbricaded design of overlapping feathers seen here was popular for generations. In fact, Egyptian costume resisted significant change for almost three thousand years, longer than any national dress in history.

the court of Akhenaten, the heretic king, and that of his successor, the short-reigned Tutankhamen, had a passion for a short, snappily cut wig dressed in the Nubian fashion. Otherwise, it was as if the Egyptians were saying to their Mediterranean neighbors: "We are here; we have always been here; and we shall always be here; therefore, we take no interest in these passing novelties."

Egyptian court etiquette required that mere mortals lower their eyes and keep them lowered in the presence of Pharaoh. This was probably a fortunate thing, for many of the Near Eastern emissaries would have been hard put to know where to look without going into shock. The happy, hedonistic near nakedness of the Egyptians must have seemed luridly indecent to the Asiatic ambassadors laboring under the burden of heavy robes and repressive sexual mores.

Unlike Egypt, which maintained its ethnic and political stability for three thousand years, Mesopotamia was constantly subject to invasion. Kingdoms would rise, extend their influence through the Land of the Two Rivers, become rich, complacent, and soft, then fall to a new wave of barbarians sweeping down from the hills. The Sumerians were conquered by the Akkadians, who in turn were swept aside by the dynasties of Lagash, Isin, Larsa, and Babylon. The Kassites ruled for about five-hundred years and fell to the warlike Assyrians. The Hittites founded

a great empire to the north in Anatolia; the Aramaeans and Syrians built strong states in the Levant; and the buffer zones were filled by a host of minor kingdoms under the patronage of one of the great powers.

Mesopotamian civilization was quite unlike that of Egypt. Egyptians believed in a moral and cosmic order, in just and merciful gods who bestowed immortality on their devotees. Mesopotamian religions were gloomy and pessimistic. The universe, as they saw it, was cursed with chaos. There was no sure and certain hope of a glorious afterlife; the souls of ordinary men existed for a few generations as spiteful, chittering demon-ghosts, then vanished utterly. Only kings or great heroes who had made a name for themselves were admitted to the company of the gods to feast throughout eternity. This belief alone explains why Mesopotamian cultures placed such unremitting emphasis on rank, fame, and social status.

The position of women also differed greatly in the two areas. Egyptian women had an unusual degree of personal freedom and independence. In fact, the custom of marriage between brother and sister, so objectionable to the modern world, was instituted because Egypt was essentially matrilinear: inheritance, whether of the crown itself or merely of property, descended through the female. In the Near East, women did not inherit property, they *were* property. Apparently the Sumerian ladies of the third millennium had a certain amount of freedom and status, but from there on it was downhill all the way. The decent married women of Assyria and Babylon were kept under wraps and veiled; but harlots who dared to assume the veil were "beaten fifty stripes with rods, and pitch was poured on their heads," a punishment that could seriously interfere with their professional careers.

Nudity and near nudity were considered shameful. Among the Sumerians, goddesses and heroes were often depicted unclothed, but in the Assyro-Babylonian epoch, nakedness served to identify slaves or female demons and had strong overtones of shame and degradation.

The long Sumerian robe remained in style in Mesopotamia for many centuries, but was gradually replaced by a long or medium-length sewn tunic with short sleeves worn with or without a girdle. This was the sole garment of the working classes; the wealthy and well-born added a second tunic and layers of shawls, shoulder capes, and cloaks, all heavily fringed and embroidered. Costumes for men and women were virtually identical, women's shawls being a bit fuller and more loosely draped. The Babylonians were obsessed with social status, and elaborate costumes were worn by the king and high priests. For great ceremonies the king wore a deeply fringed shawl, shaped like a long triangle, that wound around his body many times and was draped so that only the fringe showed. Ordinarily he wore a smaller shawl that spiraled around three times, with the end brought over the right shoulder.

When the Assyrian swept down like a wolf on the fold, his cohorts gleamed not only in purple and gold, but also in glittering, scaly iron armor. The Assyrians did not invent ironworking, but they were certainly the first people of the ancient world to exploit it. Theirs was a military state, and their greatest contribution to costume lay in the development of arms and armor. Assyrian soldiers wore tunics, prob-

The peoples of Mesopotamia, more prudish and more status conscious than the Egyptians, eschewed the revealing loincloth in favor of a flowing tunic (above) that often reached the wearer's ankles. Short tunics in simpler fabrics (below) were worn by soldiers, laborers, and common citizens. The bas-relief at upper right provides a rare glimpse of Assyrian domestic life. It shows King Ashurbanipal and his wife dining alfresco.

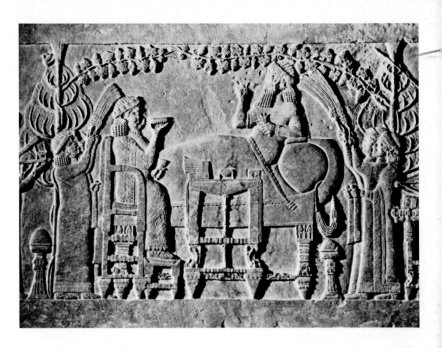

ably of leather, often plated all over with small pieces of iron overlapping like the scales of a fish. On their heads they wore pointed helmets of boiled leather or bronze. By the late Assyrian period, they also had high boots that laced up the front over shin guards. Officers had the additional protection of a mail hood covering their necks and plated tunics falling to the ankle that combined protection and rank.

Assyrian formal costume was largely taken from the Babylonians. The king wore a long, embroidered short-sleeved tunic of fine wool or linen. A second, heavier tunic was worn over that, and the outfit was topped off with either the draped Babylonian shawl or with a long, oval poncho fastened somewhere at the sides to hold it more closely to the body. The garments dripped with fringe and were encrusted with embroidery. Mesopotamian embroidery, generally called "Babylonian work," was famous throughout the ancient world and must have been magnificent to see. None of it has survived, but sculptures and bas-reliefs of the period give a reasonably accurate picture. Courtiers dressed similarly to the king, but not so elaborately. The military insistence on visible symbols of rank carried over into civilian life. Status was indicated by strict attention to minute details—the color, the precise width of embroidered edgings, the depth of the fringe, and the richness of the material.

Little is known of Assyrian female costume; woman's place was in the harem, not on monuments. A noted exception is the wife of Ashurbanipal (king of Assyria 669–626 B.C.), who is shown dining with her lord in the garden. The king reclines on a couch, his heavily embroidered tunic half-covered by a lap robe, his intricately curled and oiled hair held in place by a headband. The queen's garments are similar to his. She wears a long-sleeved, embroidered dress with a matching fringed shawl around her lower body, the end draped across her shoulders. The couple is attended by beardless servants—possibly eunuchs—who wear long robes with deep fringe but no embroidery.

To the northwest of Egypt, in Homer's wine-dark sea, lay the island of Crete with its flourishing Minoan civilization. If the manners,

Overleaf: Priests and priestesses of Minoan Crete decorate the side of a sarcophagus. The former wear long skirts with tails— the kaunakes of Mesopotamia. The latter are clad in typically Cretan robes, fitted through the bodice and embroidered.

social structure, and costumes of the Egyptians shocked the Near Easterners, those of the Minoans would have embarrassed them even more. The society of Crete was probably matriarchal in structure. Certainly Minoan women enjoyed personal freedom and the advantages of individual status. In the world of commerce or the world of the royal court, in the shrines, or in the arenas for the quasi-sacred bull dance, women pursued their own careers, apparently the equals of men.

Almost alone among the civilizations of antiquity, the Minoans seemed immune to the curse of militarism. The only major military endeavor in Minoan tradition, an attempted invasion of Sicily, ended in disaster and no doubt left the island open to the Mycenaean invasion that ended the autonomy of the kingdom. Perhaps the absence of a strong military tradition accounts for the apparent lack of interest in outward symbols of rank. Status existed in Minoan culture as it does in all societies, but the Minoans were not obsessed with it, nor was their society rigidly stratified. The throne room, still preserved in the ruins of Knossos tells the story best. Minos, the king, sat on a throne as one would expect, a majestic throne with a high back and a seat thoughtfully curved to fit his exalted bottom. His councillors also sat, admittedly on flat backless benches along the walls—but the point is, they sat. Such an action would have been inconceivable in any of the royal assemblies of the Near East or Egypt.

Minoan Crete was a maritime culture. For approximately seven centuries (2100–1400 B.C.), the Minoans dominated eastern Mediterranean trade. Although their country was small, their economy placed them on a level of near equality with Egypt and Babylon. Minoans, identified as *Keftiu*, are shown in tomb paintings bringing tribute to Pharaoh, but this probably is one of those diplomatic compliments so dear to the ancient world. Secure on a small island, protected by a huge fleet, the Minoans were comparatively free from the threat of invasion and conquest.

Male costume was simple and elegant. Men wore a brief loincloth of patterned fabric, shaped to a point in front and held in at the waist by a tight belt, often decorated with rosettes or spirals in silver or gold. For journeys or outdoor work, they wore soft leather boots tightly fitted to the legs. A second type of loincloth was worn for sports and strenuous activity. It consisted of a brief, diaperlike covering, possibly of leather, with a short apron in the rear that barely covered the buttocks and with an intriguingly erotic bulge in front.

Women's costume was equally elegant, but far from simple. The standard design was a long, bell-shaped skirt and a tight bodice. Following this basic pattern, Minoan women let their imaginations run free and came up with a surprising number of variations. It might be claimed that they invented dressmaking in the modern sense of the word. Minoan goddess figurines in either ivory or ceramic wear skirts that are heavily flounced, pleated, tucked, or in a number of other ways embellished.

Dresses may have been composed of several successively shorter skirts, worn one over the other, but more likely the effect was achieved by gathering lengths of material and sewing them onto a foundation so

that the hem of each flounce fell over the head of the one below it. Over the skirt a short apron was sometimes worn, cut very high at the sides but falling approximately to the knees front and back. The waist was pulled in by a broad, tight belt, probably of leather, similar to those worn by the men. A bodice with elbow-length sleeves was worn on the upper body, very closely fitted but cut away in front from the shoulders leaving the breasts entirely bare. For the timid, blouses were available in transparent linen. Bright colors were favored and both bodice and skirt were richly ornamented with braid and embroidery. Women wore their hair long, twisted and piled into intricate loops and curls. Many of the Minoan figurines that have been found wear tall, fantastic hats. Jewelery and cosmetics were popular and worn by men as well as women. The overall effect was sophisticated, seductive, and utterly charming.

The Mycenaeans, the aggressive invaders of mainland Greece and the eventual conquerors of Crete, adopted Minoan costume, but with certain reservations. Men favored stiff boxer shorts, possibly cut from leather, rather than the Cretan loincloth or codpiece. Female costume, obviously patterned after the Minoan, seems somehow stiffer and less flowing, although this aspect may merely be the result of conventions followed by Mycenaean artists.

When Homer spoke of Mycenae "rich in gold," he was not merely indulging in poetic license. The beehive tombs at that site had been thoroughly looted during antiquity, but the shaft graves, located in a sacred circle close inside the Lion Gate, yielded a staggering amount of treasure—cups, rhytons, diadems, rings, and several hundred large sequins. The last-mentioned item, disks of thin gold, was ornamented with patterns of flowers or sea creatures in repoussé and pierced to be sewn on festive robes. Mycenaean great ladies must have positively clanked as they walked through the winding streets of their hilltop fortresses.

After the fall of Crete, around 1400 B.C., the Mycenaeans, like the Minoans before them, became masters of the Mediterranean. Mycenaean supremacy lasted for about two hundred years, then fell as a result of some overwhelming disaster, usually identified with the semi-legendary Trojan War. While the Achaeans (or Mycenaeans) seemingly won that war, Homer does not paint a picture of unqualified success. The Achaean armies were decimated by plague and many great heroes were killed in battle. Often, the Greeks who did return home—like Agamemnon and Odysseus—returned to face death, destruction, or rebellion in their own cities. Legend attempted to deal poetically with brutal reality. Historical fact suggests that what actually took place was an abortive raid against Egypt during the late Empire period. The Achaeans and the other sea peoples allied with them were soundly defeated. The Mycenaean kingdoms never recovered. A marked decline set in. Less wealth was seen in the cities. Many of the naval bases and trading posts were abandoned. The commerce of the eastern Mediterranean fell into other hands. When the end finally came around 1100 B.C. with the savage invasion by the Dorian Greeks, it came to an already dying civilization.

3

The Classical World

Like the Egyptians before them, the ancient Greeks demonstrated a clear preference for simple clothes and immutable designs. The salient features of Attic costume were that it was essentially shapeless, that it made no accommodation to the wearer's size or sex, and that it was always draped, never cut or fitted. The vase painting detail opposite shows enthroned Zeus clad in the classic himation with Hermes wearing the chlamys over a brief kilt. The goddesses in his retinue wear the peplos, a belted robe that falls to the ankles.

INTO THE DECLINING MYCENAEAN KINGDOMS swarmed a horde of uninvited guests, the Dorians. Like the Mycenaeans, the Dorians were Greek-speaking and descended from the same ethnic stock that had produced the earlier civilization. But the Dorians had existed on the fringes of the Mycenaean world, uninfluenced by the sophisticated culture of Crete. Savage, illiterate barbarians, greedy for land and gold, the Dorians spread through Greece like a flood, leaving behind them a path of total destruction. Scornful of cities, they pillaged and burned them; despising the arts of civilization, they destroyed what they did not understand. Thus began the Dark Ages of Greece, a period of cultural decline lasting from about 1100 to 800 B.C.—an inauspicious beginning for one of the most brilliant artistic and intellectual cultures the world has ever known, that of classical Greece.

During the time of troubles, Mycenaean refugees fled to Ionia, where the Dorians had not yet penetrated, or to the great walls of the Athenian acropolis, where the invaders had been repulsed. As time passed, a new civilization emerged based on remnants of the old Mycenaean culture, leavened by the advanced cultures of the Ionian mainland, and transformed by the restless vitality of the Dorians.

Like Greek civilization, Greek costume evolved out of a combination of Doric and Ionic elements. Pure Doric costume survived well into the fifth century in conservative Sparta, where it appealed to the Spartans' rustic virtues. The garments consisted of rectangular lengths of woolen fabric that could be draped about the body in various ways.

The basic costume for men was the exomis, a plain strip of cloth fastened on the left shoulder to leave the right arm free. Usually belted at the waist and falling to about mid-thigh, it permitted great freedom of movement and could easily be discarded for heavy or dirty work. That working men are often shown naked in Greek vase painting is to be understood as a fact of everyday life, rather than as an artistic convention. Over the exomis men often wore a long woolen robe, the himation, which was not pinned or fastened, but merely draped around the body in various ways and tucked in at the waist to stay in place. Men of the upper class and the intelligentsia often wore it as their only garment, for the exomis had distinct working-class overtones. For journeys or for military activity, men wore a short, rectangular cape, the chlamys, in place of the himation.

Over many centuries the Attic sun has bleached the color from these draped figures, but the essential lines remain—a three-dimensional catalog of changing Athenian fashion. At right, a kore of the Archaic period wearing an embroidered himation over an Ionic chiton of dyed, finely woven linen. Above, the famed Caryatids supporting the Erechtheum porch atop the Acropolis. They also wear the Ionic chiton, adopted in 558 B.C. and generally cut from linen instead of wool. As the bas-relief at left indicates, the latter garment was considerably fuller than its Doric predecessor.

Women's costume was equally uncomplicated. Doric women wore the peplos, a long robe made of the usual blanketlike piece of cloth, reaching from the shoulder to the ankle with a generous overfold at the top falling to the waist. At the shoulders it was caught and held by two large pins. It could be belted at the waist, sewn up the side, or, in Spartan fashion, left open on the right side. Athenians professed to be shocked by the bare-thighed Spartan women, calling them nymphomaniacs. Not so; as children, Spartan girls exercised naked with the boys and as grown women enjoyed a degree of self-reliance and independence unknown to the more sheltered women of Athens. Such insults from ignorant foreigners could be disdainfully ignored.

Athenian women also wore the peplos in the archaic period, but with a difference. Their garments were narrower and modestly sewn up the side seam, as seen in many vase paintings of the sixth century. Spartan ladies probably wore a peplos of plain, unbleached wool, perhaps with a narrow ornamental border; but the Athenian and Ionian women reveled in luxuriously patterned weaving and embroidery. They preferred geometric patterns, the favorite design being a checkerboard with rosettes, crosses, firewheels, palmettes, or stylized animals in alternate squares. The meander, or Greek key, was used along borders.

Athenian women were not allowed to retain their Doric peplos for long. In 558 B.C. the Athenians were defeated in a military venture against Aegina; only one man lived to tell the tale. The Athenian women, outraged that he still lived while so many others lay dead on the field of battle, attacked him and stabbed him to death with the long, daggerlike pins they used to fasten their gowns. According to Herodotus, the Athenian men were more horrified at this murder than at the loss of their entire army. To punish the women, it was decreed that they should lay aside the Doric style and wear instead the Ionic chiton, foregoing such potentially dangerous trinkets. As a patriotic gesture the women of Aegina and those of Argos, its ally, retained the Doric gown and made their dress pins half again as long and lethal.

In fact, Ionic costume had long been popular on the mainland. The main difference between the two styles lay in the fabric itself. While Doric costume was of good, honest wool, the Ionic was of fine, thin linen. In other respects, the costumes of both areas were similar, made of the same flat pieces of cloth with local variations in seaming and draping. The Ionic chiton was much more voluminous than the Doric peplos, sometimes as much as nine feet wide, and always sewn down the side. Slits for the arms were left at the top, not the sides of the garment, which was caught together at intervals along the upper arm by seaming or by tiny brooches or studs. It was then tied at the waist by a narrow cord and the upper part was pulled out over the cord to give a blouselike effect.

An alternative way of controlling the drape of the material was to use a longer cord crossed between the breasts and looped at the back and under the arms before tying. This brought the garment closer to the body and permitted the arms greater freedom of movement. Tied and draped properly, it gave the effect of sleeves. The linen used for this graceful dress was thin and more or less transparent. A heavier cloak was often worn over it, passing under the left arm and fastened along the upper right. The cloak had a wide ornamental border and was occasionally embroidered in an all-over pattern. This costume can be seen to perfection in vase paintings of the archaic period, or on the lovely *korai*, the votive maidens of the Athenian Acropolis.

Young men of good family wore similar garments on formal occasions, just as suggestively transparent and as delicately embroidered. No doubt the city elders lamented this trend toward sybaritic luxury. A philosopher, seeing a group of young men thus splendidly attired, snarled, "Affectation!" Then seeing a band of Spartans, laconically draped in deliberately shabby robes, he added: "More affectation!"

The Greeks loved fine clothes and made use of intricate methods of draping to express their individual personalities; yet, on the whole, they were body conscious rather than clothes conscious. They exercised naked in the gymnasium, and they competed naked in the games. Some sort of costume, probably the exomis, appears to have been worn in the earlier games, but in the fifteenth Olympiad in 720 B.C. the contestants appeared without clothing. The only sport requiring a traditional costume was chariot racing. For this a long, belted chiton was worn, as seen in the famous bronze sculpture of the *Charioteer of Delphi.*

A fine, well-developed body was prized above all worldly goods, and a great deal of time and effort went into cultivating and maintaining it. Even men who had neither the ambition nor the talent to star in the games worked out religiously from childhood on. Along with the study of music and poetry, physical education was one of the main features of the schooling of the Greek gentleman. Classical Greece was probably the only culture known where complete nudity was acceptable at a formal dinner or at a symposium—a drinking party —provided, of course, that the man in question had the figure to carry it off. Such a display might have been felt to indicate an unhealthy amount of pride, but it would not have been considered indecent.

Other Mediterranean nations would have found it hard to understand this attitude, which, for that matter, had not always prevailed in Greece itself. As Plato remarked: "It is not so long ago that the Hellenes, like most barbarians, regarded the naked man as something shocking and ludicrous." Certainly the Persians never understood the Greeks. What was worse, they made the mistake of underestimating them. When Darius sent a huge force to Marathon, it never occurred to him that he would be defeated by the small band of Athenians and Plataeans drawn up to oppose him. When Xerxes attempted his invasion some years later, he moved at the head of an army that, according to Herodotus, drank whole lakes and rivers dry in its passing. Yet he, too, learned his lesson the hard way, in defeat at Salamis and Plataea. In many of the Greek monuments of the fifth century, Persians joined the ranks of traditional enemies of the Greeks—Titans, mythological centaurs, and Trojans—who allegorically represent barbarism and tyranny brought to heel by Greek intellect and independence.

Persian costume was different from any in the Mediterranean cultures so far discussed. Sumerians, Egyptians, Assyro-Babylonians, and Greeks all made their attire from lengths of fabric draped around

The ancient Greeks were body conscious to a degree unparalleled among civilized societies. They exercised, bathed in public, and competed on the athletic fields stark naked. In fact, the only athletic costume in all of Greece was the chiton worn for chariot racing (below). Although Persia lay just across the Aegean Sea from Greece, it developed its distinctive national costume (right) from central Asian rather than from Attic antecedents.

their bodies with a minimum of sewing. The Minoans alone made extensive use of seaming and dressmaking, but their costume style died out in the chaos of the Dorian invasions and their aftermath. The Persians were heirs to a totally different tradition of dress. Their ancestors were horsemen out of the plains of central Asia, the home of tailored and fitted garments of felt and leather.

Original Persian costume consisted of an open, knee-length coat and fairly wide trousers, usually cut in several pieces, since the patterns had to be adapted to the size of the available hides. At the time of the Persian Wars, such basic outfits were still being worn by outlying tribes of barbarian horsemen—Parthians, Scythians, or Sarmatians— but the Persians themselves had borrowed elements from the Medes and Babylonians, thus evolving a more sophisticated national style.

The basic Achaemenid costume consisted of long, wide trousers gathered at the waist and tapering to the ankles; a long-sleeved tunic was worn with the pants and belted over them at the waist. Both tunic and pants were made of soft wools or medium-weight linen. In sculptures and vase paintings the fabric is shown draping gracefully. Over the tunic, Persians wore a long coat with fitted, set-in sleeves. It was often worn hanging off the shoulders and tied at the neck, with the sleeves falling free. Soft, low boots or shoes were worn and a wide variety of hats. Kings wore the long, flowing Median robe of honor, a rectangular sewn garment, unfitted and voluminous, pulled over the head and belted to give the effect of large, flowing sleeves. Color was used lavishly and costumes were enriched with embroidery or tapestry-woven bands of decoration.

The Persians did not force their costume onto their subject peoples. The great Achaemenid kings were masters of many nations, and the varieties of national dress seen at royal assemblies must have been a pleasant reminder of that fact. The beautifully carved ceremonial staircase at Persepolis shows all manner of men come to pay tribute. Some bring articles of clothing as gifts. The delegation from Parthia bring sleeved coats and long, narrow trousers with feet attached, perhaps the world's first leotards. In the seventh book of his histories, Herodotus describes at length the military costume of the Persians and their allies—Medes, Cissians, Assyrians, Lydians, Bactrians, and many others. As far as the Greeks were concerned, they were all barbarians, all had been defeated, and most of them wore pants.

The classical Greeks and their successors in the Mediterranean never deviated from the firm opinion that draped robes identify the civilized man, while pants are worn by barbarians. But the Greeks had no objection whatever to some of the more opulent aspects of semi-Oriental attire—rich, deep colors, even royal purples; increasing use of gold thread and ornament; and the new luxury fabric, silk, which began to be seen in Athens during the Age of Pericles.

Greek fashions became quite complicated after the Persian Wars. On the one hand, there was an influx of foreign luxury goods, and on the other, an upsurge of nationalism revived the popularity of the Doric peplos. The Ionic chiton came back into favor in the fourth century, perhaps as a result of anti-Spartan sentiment engendered by the Peloponnesian Wars. The chiton was draped, tied, and fastened in various complicated ways and often combined with Doric elements, like the deep overfold at the top, with the himation artfully draped over all. The conquests of Alexander in the late fourth century B.C. made foreign costume more acceptable; women are frequently shown wearing semifitted gowns with long, tight sleeves embroidered and ornamented in the Persian fashion.

Greek style, like Alexander, conquered the world. Alexander himself had been fired by a vision of one world, an empire of cultural as well as political unity. But at his death, the political unity of his vast empire collapsed into new patterns of emerging Hellenistic kingdoms ruled by Macedonian dynasties—the Ptolemys in Egypt, the Seleucids in Syria, and the Antigonids in Greece, while a host of minor kingdoms took up the slack in between. Yet throughout the Hellenistic world a rising tide of Greek cultural influence swamped the venerable cultures of Egypt and the Near East. Alexandria, Antioch, Pergamon, Sardis, Ephesus, all were basically Greek cities with Greek language, religion, customs, and general culture superimposed onto indigenous traditions. Only an Alexander—brash, ambitious, himself only half-civilized—would have presumed to reject the ideals of civilizations far older than Greece and to substitute Hellenism in their place. And perhaps only the ancient Near East, accustomed to the tradition of divine kingship, would have been overawed by his larger-than-life personality into accepting it.

Throughout the eastern Mediterranean, wealthy and fashionable men and women, no matter what their backgrounds, spoke, thought, and dressed Greek. Back in Athens, which was sliding rapidly into a condition of shabby gentility, philosophers in the plain Doric himation came and went talking of the past glories of the Age of Pericles.

Meanwhile, in the western Mediterranean, a conflict was brewing that was to decide the fate of the Western world. Many civilizations had emerged and declined in the Aegean, while to the west the Italian peninsula lay shrouded in obscurity. By 1000 B.C. Italic-speaking peoples had begun to drift in successive waves into the central and southern parts of Italy, where they made permanent settlements. One such tribe, speaking the Latin dialect, settled along the western coast on the Tiber River and later came to form the heart of the strongest and most stable empire known to Western civilization.

Roman civilization was slow to develop. During the formative years (700 to 350 B.C.), the Romans were overshadowed by the Etruscan kingdoms to the north of Rome and by the Greek city-states to the south. Both the Etruscans and Greeks were culturally superior to the agrarian Romans, whom they very likely considered little better than barbarians. Traditionally the Romans dated the foundation of their city to 753 B.C., but during the early centuries of its growth, Rome was subject to Etruscan influence and domination. Etruscan kings ruled Rome until 509 B.C. when the last of them, Tarquin the Proud, was driven out and Roman independence proclaimed.

Etruscan origins are obscure, but recent archaeological evidence indicates a Near Eastern source. Their costume, like their culture, was

At its height the Persian Empire stretched from the Indus to the Mediterranean and from the Indian Ocean to the Caucasus. Dozens of captive nations came under the sway of Persia's great kings—Cyrus, Darius, Xerxes—and each sent tribute-bearing emissaries to Persepolis every year. The bas-relief detail above shows those representatives in their varied national finery and traditional headgear.

eclectic, consisting of a combination of Greek and Asiatic elements together with details peculiarly Etruscan. In the archaic period, women wore gowns showing unmistakable Near Eastern influence: long dresses, with half-length sleeves, fitted tightly to the upper part of the body and flaring out in the skirt. Details of seaming are not clear. The sleeves for example, seem to be cut in one piece with the body of the dress, which would have resulted in a shocking waste of fabric. Perhaps the fullness of the skirt was achieved by inset gores. The gown was high in the neck and open down the back, where it was fastened with ribbons and worn unbelted.

The timeless rapture of the dance absorbs the two figures at left, who gambol across the wall of an Etruscan tomb. Both wear versions of the tebenna, a semicircular cloak that was the forerunner of the Roman toga. The tebenna came in a variety of lengths and colors, and patterned borders were common.

For variation, an overblouse of heavier material reaching to the hips might be worn over the gown. The material used was linen or lightweight wool; many of the costumes shown in the tomb paintings of Tarquinia are quite transparent. Some dresses were embroidered with an all-over pattern of tiny dots or floral motifs; all had bands of decorative braid or embroidery at the hem, neckline, and sleeves. Women usually wore a cloak over the dress, a plain rectangle of wool draped over the shoulders and sometimes covering the head.

Etruscan men of this period wore a version of the fitted tunic with short cap sleeves. Older men wore the tunic long, down to mid-calf,

while young men cut it so short it barely covered their behinds. The longer tunics were often decorated with clavi, vertical borders in strong contrasting colors. This ornament carried over into Roman costume, where it indicated rank and status. Over the tunic they wore the distinctive Etruscan cloak, the tebenna, a semicircular scarf that became the prototype for the Roman toga. Often the tebenna was worn alone without the tunic, draped carelessly over the arms. Like the women, the men favored sheer fabrics. Both sexes loved strong and lively colors—rich blues, greens, reds, and yellows. Instead of sandals, they usually wore soft boots with pointed, turned-up toes, probably the most distinctively Near Eastern feature of Etruscan costume, indicating a central Anatolian origin.

Etruscan jewelry was sensational and doubtless contributed to the early tales of Etruscan luxury, so detested by the early impoverished Romans. Etruscan tombs have yielded necklaces, brooches, diadems, bracelets, rings, and other ornaments of every description and purpose. Their artisans worked in gold, using highly advanced techniques of repoussé and granulation. The Etruscans' treasures were buried with them in the carved and painted tombs of Cerveteri and Tarquinia. The pleasures of this life were thought to be repeated in the next, an eternity of feasting, drinking, dancing, and music-making in olive groves and

The Roman toga, which began as a strictly utilitarian garment that could be worn by any adult, evolved into a ceremonial robe of such complexity and moment that it was seldom worn except on state occasions. Toga draping was an art in itself, and powerful Romans such as Emperor Tiberius (above) employed servants exclusively for that purpose. When offering a sacrifice to the gods (above left), noble Romans drew a fold of the toga over their heads as a gesture of piety. In wartime the toga was abandoned in favor of the sewn linen tunic, which was worn under the armor (right).

vineyards, or reclining on couches built for two while being served by beautiful naked boys.

In the late fourth century and in the third, much of the exuberance and vitality seems to have drained out of Etruscan art and life. The old vivid costumes were abandoned; the tomb paintings show sad-eyed couples resigned to their fate, wearing costumes that are almost direct copies of the Greek. The husband still hands his wife an egg, the symbol of eternal life, but now the gesture lacks joy and hope. Demons of the underworld are frequently pictured, and the view of the after-life becomes increasingly pessimistic. They must have known by then that they were a people without a future. Exhausted by wars with the Gauls and local Italic tribes, they were conquered by the Romans and their sophisticated culture was wiped out. The Romans then performed the final insult of blackening their reputation to posterity, picturing them as lascivious, heartless tyrants, steeped in blood and gold.

The plain truth is that the Romans owed much of their culture to the Etruscans and didn't like to be reminded of that embarrassing fact. Roman religion, in particular, was derived from Etruria, for all of its superficial resemblance to the Greek pantheon; and Roman architecture, which at first glance seems to derive from Greek prototypes, can also be traced to Etruscan sources. Throughout much of their early history, the Romans had distinct feelings of cultural inferiority. Once the Greek city-states of southern Italy had been subjugated, the Romans absorbed Greek culture and became as Hellenized as possible. But while broad, Roman Hellenization was not deep; it was at best like the lavish sheets of fine-colored marble veneer that covered the sturdy buildings made from honest, homely Roman brick.

Roman costume was eclectic. It took the tebenna from the Etruscans, enlarged and transformed it into the toga. Women borrowed the Greek chiton and himation, modified into the stola and palla. The Roman army went so far as to steal the trousers from the Gauls and reissue them as standard military equipment. The Romans were thus the first Mediterranean people to adopt this particular item of barbarian attire. Yet for all this persistent borrowing from various sources, even perhaps because of it, the Romans developed a style entirely their own.

The toga, the most distinctive of all Roman garments, was heavy with symbolic meaning. Only citizens who had voting rights could wear it; color and decoration were carefully regulated according to status. Freeborn sons of citizens started out in life wrapped in the *toga praetexta*, white with a band of scarlet or purple along the straight edge. At the age of sixteen, the boy became a man and inherited the plain *toga virilis* of natural, unbleached wool. He could earn his stripe again only through a lifetime of service and dedication to the state. In the adult world, the purple stripe designated senators and magistrates. Candidates for office wore the *toga candida*, bleached to a dazzling white that symbolized the purity of their intentions. Effeminates and fashion faddists with no sense of shame wore the *toga vitrea*—as its name indicates, you could see through it like glass. The *toga pulla*, black or dark colored, was worn by mourners. Augurs and certain priests wore the *toga trabea*, decorated with a scarlet stripe and purple hem.

Victorious generals, and later on emperors and consuls, were awarded the *toga picta*, dyed a rich purple and heavily embroidered with gold.

The cut and draping of the garment went through several stages that parallel the growth and decline of the fortunes of Rome itself. During the Republic, the toga was a simple, uncomplicated all-purpose wrap, the main garment of the austere Roman by day and his blanket by night. Its prototype, however, was the Etruscan tebenna, not the Greek himation. It was cut as a semicircle rather than as a rectangle and in this early period was of moderate size. As the republic expanded into an empire, the toga expanded until it measured twenty feet in length and seven to ten feet in depth at its widest part.

Roman women wore costumes based on Greek attire: the draped and belted Ionic chiton was renamed the stola, the himation became the palla. Their love of luxury was reflected in their preference for rich and exotic fabrics such as the rare silks worn (below, left, and center) at a time when the costly import was, theoretically at least, forbidden by law.

The draping of the toga was complex: first, it was folded lengthwise down the middle, then thrown over the left shoulder so that about a third of it hung down in front. The rest was brought across the back, then under the right arm and around again to the front, where the remaining end was thrown backward over the left shoulder. Somewhere along the way, folds were rolled and twisted at the waist to give a belted effect, and a portion of the innermost drape was pulled up over it to form the characteristic small pouch of drapery to the left of the waistline. Correct draping of the toga became so intricate that wealthy men had a slave whose sole chore in life was to get his master in and out of this cumbrous costume. As Tertullian groaned: "This is no garment, but a burden."

Officials continued to wear the toga as late as the fifth century A.D. and found it, no doubt, not the least onerous of their public charges. But by then the awkward garment had shrunk to a mere six feet or less in width, doing away with the need for the longitudinal fold. The average Roman citizen had virtually given up on it altogether, wearing it on particularly festive occasions, then laying it away to be buried in.

The toga was never worn by itself, as was the himation. By comparison with the Greeks, middle- and upper-class Romans wore a lot of clothing. For underwear the Romans wore a sewn loincloth and a short, sleeveless subtunic, usually of linen. Over this they wore the tunic, a garment made of two pieces of material sewn up the sides and across the shoulders. It was pulled over the head, tied at the waist, and fell just above the knees. Men of rank wore it under the toga. By itself, it was the costume of the common people. Like the toga, it went through several stylistic modifications. The original tunic had short cap sleeves, produced by the normal drape of the material. The sleeves had crept down to the elbow by the time of Augustus, who was unusually sensitive to cold; according to Suetonius, he wore as many as four tunics plus extra underwear. Commodus, in the late second century A.D., introduced full-length sleeves. During the third century, the tunic grew longer, reaching to just above the ankle. In the Republic and early Empire, the tunic was ornamented along the side seam with clavi, vertical borders borrowed from the Etruscans. Like the toga, the width and color of the clavi were strictly regulated according to social standing.

While the toga was being gradually abandoned, other outer garments were being invented to take its place. To indicate their cultural preferences, intellectuals wore the pallium, a copy of the Greek himation. At dinner parties, fashionable men wore the synthesis, a weird combination garment that retained the simplicity of the tunic above the waist and the fullness of the toga below. A hooded cloak, the paenula, was a serviceable all-weather garment worn by men of all classes. Soldiers serving along the Gallic frontier favored the sagum, an inelegant blanket-wrap. There was also the dalmatic, a long, straight-sleeved garment, popular during the third century, which originated in Dalmatia. Richly decorated down the front with clavi, which by that time had ceased to have any symbolic meaning, it was said to have been introduced by the depraved and effeminate Heliogabalus. Oddly enough, the dalmatic became the distinctive attire of pious and un-worldly Christians during the following century.

Roman military costume was based on civilian attire, with the addition of protective coverings. Soldiers wore the usual knee-length tunic and a cloak of some kind. Heavy boots, shinguards, and a bronze helmet took care of the extremities. The middle was covered by a heavy corselet of leather and metal plates. Rank was indicated by insignia and by a greater or lesser degree of ornamentation. Barbarian trousers were adopted as early as the time of Augustus; they reached just below the knees and were called *feminilia*, an obvious mistake for *femorilia*. Some ancient humorist, possibly exasperated by this sissified indulgence, made the pun and the name stuck.

Roman women wore costumes almost indistinguishable from those of the Greeks. The Ionic chiton was renamed the stola, the himation the palla; both were worn over a sleeveless tunic similar to those worn by the men. During the Republic, no doubt, Roman matrons dressed so-berly. In the early Empire, the empress Livia attempted to maintain the austere tradition by dressing in good, honest wool—spun and woven by her own imperial hands. The gesture was in vain. Roman women loved delicate fabrics and vivid colors; they wore the finest of linens and thin, fragile cottons and silks imported from India, materials as light as the ladies' reputations. "Our women expose themselves to the world," growled one harassed and henpecked Roman, "as much as to their lover in the bedchamber." The dresses were edged with purple and em-broidered with pearls and gold spangles; rich braid and tapestrywork were sewn on at the neck and sleeves; all colors were used—blues, greens, yellows, reds and purples—in all shades and intensities. Wealthy ladies had robes that seem woven of changeable silk, purple in the shadows, gold where the light catches it.

Sumptuary laws to control this rage for foreign luxuries were constantly passed by the Senate and just as constantly ignored. The women would have their silk robes, thin as the air itself, and no one was going to stop them. There was a very real problem involved. Roman lawmakers were not motivated solely by crusty chauvinism. The far-off, almost unknown kingdoms of India, which supplied the muslins and acted as middlemen for the Chinese silks, were totally un-interested in any of the raw materials offered by the Romans as trade in kind. They wanted cold hard cash. As a result, there was during the Empire a constant drain of Roman gold into the rich cities of southern India. Most of the trade was carried out by the merchants of Arabia Felix or Ethiopia, who controlled the Indian Ocean.

Unlike the Egyptians and the Greeks, and despite their love of sheer silk and other see-through fabric, the Romans were clothes conscious rather than body conscious. They spent hours on baths, cosmetics, and coiffures, but they stressed in their attire gorgeous materials and ornaments rather than the body underneath. Roman male costume showed the same orientation. The Greek philosopher in his simple himation displayed the fine body that he kept in good condition well into middle age; his deliberately understated garments spoke quietly of high thinking and plain living. The huge Roman toga, swamping

Romans of both sexes gave considerable time and attention to their morning toilet. During the Empire men took to wearing make-up and perfume and crimping their locks in the imperial manner. Women, following the lead of the profligate empress Messalina, spent hours on their grooming (right), much of it devoted to intricate coiffures (above) augmented by false switches, chignons, and full or partial wigs crafted from the blond hair of barbarian slaves.

the wearer in vast, unwieldy but majestic folds, boasted openly of power, prestige, and grandeur.

The toga was the outward symbol of Roman *gravitas*, the qualities of austerity, honesty, conservatism, and devotion to civic duty that built a city-state into a republic and the republic into an empire. The abandonment of the garment was seen by concerned critics as an omen of the decline of Rome itself. By the third century A.D., Rome had become an enormous, indolent parasite gorging on the wealth of conquered nations. Roman coinage was debased and devalued as it flowed eastward to purchase luxuries. More money was needed to equip armies raised against the new Persian empire of the Sassanians and the hordes of barbarians exerting relentless pressure along the Roman borders. The army itself had to be maintained by the recruitment of ex-policemen, slaves, gladiators, criminals, and barbarians, as Romans had lost interest in military careers. In 212 A.D., the emperor Caracalla extended full Roman citizenship to all free individuals of the empire, since as citizens they automatically fell into a higher tax bracket. All sorts of foreigners now wore the toga, and Romans lost interest in that too.

Constantine the Great, in the early fourth century A.D., initiated a series of reforms intended to preserve the empire. He legalized and encouraged Christianity in the hope that it would restore the moral values that had contributed to the greatness of Rome. He moved his capital to his new city of Constantinople where the military situation was most acute. At his death, he devided the empire between his two sons, one ruling in the east, the other in the west. These decisions had far-reaching effects on the future of Europe. When the fifth century dawned, the Eastern Empire had been firmly drawn into the Oriental world; the Western Empire was staggering under the onslaught of Germanic barbarians; and a third power, the Christian church, was making ready to reconquer the Western world in the name of Rome.

4

Saints, Soldiers, and Savages

IN A.D. 410 THE MEDITERRANEAN WORLD was shaken to its foundations when a barbarian tribe, the Visigoths, captured and sacked the city of Rome. Thanks to Hollywood epics, the scene is familiar to all of us: a fierce, grizzled warrior—wearing a horned helmet and a shaggy bearskin, with a sword in one hand and a torch in the other, rampages through the Forum. Unfortunately, this picture is not very accurate.

The Gothic tribes living on the borders of the Roman Empire are commonly referred to as barbarians, but they were fairly civilized after their fashion. Their young men had long served in the Roman army, often rising to positions of great authority. They spoke the Latin language as well as their own, and, for the most part, they were Christians. They had long been associated with the Roman Empire as *foederati*, trusted allies. Around 370, these generally peaceful people were thrown into panic by the appearance on their borders of a nomadic and savage Mongolian tribe, the Huns, who swept like a whirlwind out of the eastern steppes. Terrorized, the Goths petitioned to be admitted within the Roman walls for safety.

Originally, the Goths had no intention of destroying Rome; they merely wished to share in the stability, prosperity, and security of the empire. The Romans themselves were largely to blame for their ultimate destruction. The barbarian refugees were treated with contempt by vacillating emperors and consistently ill-used by greedy border officials. Finally they rebelled. They plundered their way through Macedonia, Greece, Gaul, and Spain and, under Alaric, they ravaged Rome itself, a disaster that demoralized the Romans as nothing else could have done.

Staggering under their loot, the Goths fanned out through the Western Empire to found their own kingdoms, settling down comfortably among the remains of the Gallo-Roman civilization. But in the long run, it was the old case of the captive dominating his captor. The Roman officials, lawyers, administrators, teachers, technicians, philosophers and clergy, ushered out unceremoniously at the front door, were quietly readmitted at the back.

Roman historians of the fifth and sixth centuries recorded the appearance and costume of these invaders. They were tall, red-haired, physically powerful people, who dressed in closely fitted, sewn garments, short tunics with set-in sleeves, or sleeveless smocks that slipped over the head. They wore either short or long trousers, some of them furnished with modern-looking belt loops. Wrapped leg coverings similar to puttees were worn with short trousers; the long pants were sometimes fitted with feet. Women wore short blouses, short-sleeved or sleeveless, and full skirts gathered and tied at the waist. These garments were usually made of wool or linen; furs were worn but only for outer cloaks in cold weather. Strong, brilliant colors were popular among the wealthy, but common people made do with natural, unbleached homespun. When dyed, the wool was woven in stripes, checks, and colorful plaids. The pattern of the plaids may have identified family or clan. Actual Teutonic garments of this period have been preserved in the peat bogs of northwest Germany, Denmark, and Holland, shrouding the shrunken remains of executed criminals or victims sacrificed to the fierce northern gods.

The picture that emerges is a far cry from cinema sensationalism. But one item is correct: the horned helmet. Such helmets appear to have been worn throughout Europe from the first millennium B.C. down through the period of the invasions. They did not, however, resemble the usual cow-horn monstrosities of provincial Wagnerian Ring Cycles. Actual examples, such as the Waterloo helmet from the Thames, or the matched pair from the Danish peat bog at Vikso were crafted of handsome, heavy bronze, decorated with rosettes and spirals. The projecting metal horns were highly stylized and originally embellished with gold leaf. Great chieftains carried brilliantly gilded and ornamented shields. Both men and women wore masses of jewelry in gold, silver, and bronze—bracelets, broad collars, intricate hair ornaments, elegantly twisted torques, and huge brooches inlaid with enamel and semiprecious stones. The more Romanized of the barbarian nobility wore Mediterranean costume for great occasions. Alaric himself claimed several thousand silk robes as part of his share of Roman loot.

The barbarians had barely started to feel at home in their new kingdoms when the Huns, led by Attila, the Scourge of God, finally appeared on the stage of European history. Both the Germans and the Gallo-Romans quailed before this new menace, temporarily abandoned their own private conflicts, and united to save Western civilization from the heathen. The Huns, with their grotesquely scarred faces (ritually marked in childhood) and their well-deserved reputation for cruelty, seemed hardly human. They wore the usual central Asian pants and long, belted coats of felt and leather, topped off with cloaks made of the skins of field mice. (Either the Huns were unusually small or their mice were unusually large.) Some civilized costume was worn. Attila's women embroidered fine linens but, as the historian Priscus relates, these were worn merely to ornament barbarian clothes.

In 451, Attila was opposed by an allied army made up of Romans, Franks, Visigoths, Burgundians, and other assorted, half-civilized barbarians under the command of the Romanized Goth, Aetius. The battle was not a decisive victory for the West, but Attila was at least discouraged and withdrew. The following year he emerged from retirement long enough to invade Italy, but he died soon after. On his death, his army collapsed, fading back into the obscurity of the eastern plains.

The fall of Rome in 476 was a triumph of crudity over refinement in every respect, including costume. The barbarian invaders wore wool tunics and trousers, and they marched into battle in the horned helmets decorated with bronze plates that were the most distinctive feature of their apparel. Fabulous animals enliven the bas-relief at right.

The shattered, half-decimated Western world began to rebuild. But the Hun invasion had made one fact perfectly clear: the future of Europe had slipped away from the Romans and had fallen into the capable hands of the barbarians.

Meanwhile in the east the new Rome, Constantinople, still held out against the barbarians and continued to do so until 1453, preserving its manifold traditions inherited from Greece, Rome, and the Near East. For centuries, Constantinople was the leading commercial city of the Mediterranean basin; its strong economy insured its survival despite the pervasive aura of inefficiency, extravagance, mismanagement, and general incompetence that emanated from the Byzantine court. The golden age of Byzantium was achieved under the emperor Justinian (527–565), an extremely able ruler consumed by the ambition to restore the Roman Empire to its former greatness. He sought personal fame through three diverse paths: military conquests, building programs, and legal reforms. The reconquered lands soon fell again to the barbarians; the building programs, though magnificent, were economically debilitating; but the legal reforms established the basis of civil law throughout Europe.

Byzantine costume reflected the diverse traditions of the culture. Common people wore a blouse or tunic with short trousers and soft boots. Procopius attributed this garb to the Huns, but it could have derived from any number of Near Eastern sources. The costume of the upper classes and nobility was, naturally, as splendid and extravagant as the traffic would bear. The glittering mosaics of San Vitale, Ravenna, provide an excellent picture of gala court dress. The grave of a fifth-century empress—Maria, daughter of the barbarian general Stilicho and wife to the emperor Honorius—was opened and looted in the sixteenth century. Her golden shroud was melted down and was said to have yielded thirty-six pounds of pure gold.

Byzantine textiles were magnificent. Luxury fabrics, stiff with elab-

orate tapestrywork and embroidery, were imported from Syria, Alexandria, and Persia. Silk was imported from China but, on a limited basis, was also produced at Constantinople itself. The origin of silk had long been a mystery, although some early natural historians suggested that it was the web spun by gigantic Oriental spiders. Allegedly, sericulture was developed by a Chinese empress of the mid-third millennium B.C., the art was well developed by about 1000 B.C., and both raw yarn and finished fabrics were exported to the Western world by at least the time of Alexander. The price was nearly prohibitive.

The caravan route from China to Byzantium took approximately 250 days and passed through Persian territories where the shipments were heavily taxed. During Justinian's reign, according to the historian Procopius, silkworm eggs were smuggled out of China in the hollow

Of classical costume, Byzantium retained only the basic drapery. The vibrant colors and sumptuous fabrics in which Empress Theodora and her court are attired (left) reveal the influence of the Near East—as does the robe worn by Emperor Nicephorus Botaniates (top).

bamboo walking staffs of missionary monks. The monks must also have closely observed the complex rituals of silk farming, for the rearing of silkworms is by no means a simple matter. The Byzantines continued to import a great deal of silk, but now that China's great secret was revealed, the price went down and the rich, lustrous fabric became more widely available.

After breaking the Chinese monopoly on silk, the Byzantine emperors established their own controls and for centuries gorgeous silk garments, glittering with jewels and gold embroidery, appeared sporadically at European courts, grudging tokens of Byzantine esteem. At Constantinople and throughout the empire, color and decoration were strictly regulated according to rank and status. Common people for example, were forbidden the tablion, the purple inset in the robes of men of senatorial rank. Only the emperor and the empress were entitled to a robe entirely of purple, and only the emperor could wear hose or boots of that color. Purple fabric, colored with a rare and expensive dye obtained from shellfish, had been restricted to royalty and high-ranking personages since the time of the Babylonians. The Byzantines, moving within the strictures of the most hierarchic society the Western world has ever known, stamped on the color its final, definitive imperial meaning.

As Byzantium flourished, Rome declined. Economic decay and moral dry rot had set in early in the third century and even the reforms of Constantine were unable to do more than temporarily arrest these conditions. The Sack of Rome under Alaric had been catastrophic; Rome never recovered from this disaster and, during the Dark Ages, the city drifted ever deeper into squalid obscurity. In *The City of God*, St. Augustine interpreted this calamity as divine retribution leveled against Rome for the sins of her people, including the meek Christians who were steeped in sin, Original and otherwise, and had merely received their just deserts.

The early Church fathers preached not merely denial, but abhorrence, of the flesh—female flesh in particular—and attained amazing heights of hysterical invective. Tertullian referred to women as the devil's gateway: "The sentence of God on this sex of yours lives in this age; the guilt must of necessity live too." According to Clement of Alexandria, a woman should feel "shame even to reflect of what nature she is." He recommends that a woman should be clothed from head to foot and even veiled in public for "if thus with modesty and with a veil, she covereth her own eyes, she shall not be misled herself, nor shall she draw others by the exposure of her face, into the dangerous path of sin."

The early Christians deliberately dressed modestly and with humility, avoiding the opulent costumes that smacked of profane paganism. After the Sack of Rome, the ruined economy gave them no other choice. The wide-sleeved dalmatic was worn by men over a tight-sleeved tunic. For outerwear, they favored the pallium. Women wore the tunic and a large, oval-shaped cloak, similar to the ecclesiastical chasuble. Both men and women often decorated their tunics or dalmatics with the clavi. These broad stripes, which had once indicated high rank, were commonly used in the third and fourth centuries as a sort of livery, to identify the tunics of servants and slaves. Christians, servants of God, gladly assumed the stripes as an outward symbol of their unworldliness. Christian bodies were covered from ears to ankles in order to obscure and disguise the sinful flesh. Costumes for both sexes were cut very full from natural wool or heavy linen, unbleached and undyed. Bright, cheerful colors were avoided. As Commodian snarled, "If God had intended men to wear purple woolens, He would have created purple sheep."

Preoccupied with their souls, early Christians castigated their bodies. In those days, and throughout the Middle Ages, cleanliness was far from godliness; Christians felt with St. Jerome that "the purity of the body and its garments implies the impurity of the soul." The pagan

Romans had had entirely too much fun in those sinful, luxurious baths; Christians avoided them like the plague. The average Christian must have bathed every so often at home, but many of the early saints prided themselves on their avoidance of water except, of course, as a beverage. Anchorites wore their coarse garments until they rotted to shreds, then wove themselves tunics out of palm fibers or—so it was claimed—out of their own shaggy, uncut hair, one of the low points in the history of Western costume.

Rome, shorn of its former greatness, turned inward, seeking spiritual values. The Church increasingly dominated the social and political structure of Roman society. After the destruction of the city by the Goths, Pope Innocent I, rather than the emperor, supervised the reconstruction. When Attila threatened, it was Pope Leo I, not the emperor, who carried out negotiations in behalf of the city. St. Gregory the Great encouraged missionary activity in the barbarian north, but was equally well known for his administrative abilities at home. In effect, the authority of the pope was substituted for that of the emperor and, as the empire declined, the power of the papacy grew. Devastated, looted, half-deserted, Rome was still regarded with superstitious awe by the barbarians. Their young kingdoms looked to Rome for missionary monks and priests to minister to their spiritual and temporal needs. They were not disappointed.

The most stable of the barbarian kingdoms was that of the Franks, who had filtered across the lower Rhine in the mid-fourth century and were allowed to remain as *foederati*. Stubbornly pagan, they remained relatively uninfluenced by Rome until the late fifth century when their king, Clovis, accepted baptism. This advantageous move gained him the support both of the Gallo-Roman aristocracy of southern France and of papal Rome. Increasingly, Roman culture made its presence felt in the rude, northern kingdom although the old Germanic traditions remained strong, particularly in costume.

In contrast to the Gallo-Romans who practiced cremation, the Franks and other Germanic tribes buried their dead fully clothed and equipped for the Christian afterlife. Archaeological investigation of these graves, such as the one carried out in 1959 in the vaults of St. Denis in Paris, provide direct evidence of Merovingian costume. Queen Arnegonde (who died *c.* 570), wife of Chlotar I, had been laid there to rest in a limestone coffin lined with a bright red woolen cloak. Next to her body she wore a long-sleeved, short chemise, or shift, of fine white linen. Her overgown, or tunic, was a one-piece garment in the Romano-Byzantine style. Cut from fine, ribbed indigo-blue silk, it reached only to her knees. It also was long-sleeved and was belted low in the waist. Her legs were covered by rather baggy, white woolen stockings, held in place with leather garters. Arnegonde's most magnificent garment was a long outer robe of dark red silk lined with linen, with long full sleeves, gold embroidered at the cuffs. The short tunic was the real surprise of this find. The scarlet robe was entirely open below the waist and, standing or sitting, the royal cross-gartered legs would have been exposed. Until this discovery, it was assumed that women of this period wore concealing ankle-length gowns.

Not until Clovis, king of the Franks, permitted himself to be baptized in 496 (shown in a fourteenth-century manuscript illumination below) did the Merovingians abandon their pagan ways and embrace Roman ideas and styles. Even then they largely retained their national costume of a loose, full tunic over breeches secured by leather leg bandages.

For his coronation as Holy Roman emperor, Charlemagne—who generally avoided ostentation in dress—may have worn this magnificent silk dalmatic emblazoned with a view of Christ and the Twelve Apostles.

Under the Carolingian dynasty the Frankish kingdom considerably extended its territories. As the eighth century drew to a close, Charlemagne dominated all of Europe with the exception of the British Isles, Moslem Spain, and the wilderness beyond the Elbe and Danube rivers. On Christmas Day of the year 800 in Rome, he was crowned Holy Roman emperor by Pope Leo III. It had been three centuries since a Roman emperor had ruled in the West, but the desire for the political and cultural unity that the old empire had symbolized had not been extinguished. For the ceremony Charlemagne donned, for the sceond and last time in his life, the Roman tunic, chlamys, and shoes. He may have worn the magnificent Byzantine dalmatic still preserved at Rome in the Sacristy of St. Peter's. It is a splendid garment, made of silk, encrusted with finely embroidered scenes of Christ and the Twelve Apostles, glittering with gold scrollwork and crosses.

Strangely enough, this great king who worked so closely with the papacy and who did so much to revive Roman scholarship in the barbarian north, "despised foreign costumes, however handsome, and never allowed himself to be robed in them except twice." His biographer Einhard went on to say:

He wore the national, that is to say, the Frankish dress—next to his skin a linen shirt and linen breeches, and above these a tunic fringed in silk; hose fastened with bands covered his lower limbs, and shoes his feet; he protected his shoulders and chest in winter by a close-fitting coat of otter or marten skins. Over all he flung a blue cloak, and he always had a sword girt about him. . . . On great feast days he wore embroidered clothes and shoes studded with precious stones; his cloak was fastened by a golden buckle, and he appeared crowned with a diadem of gold and gems; but on other days his dress varied little from the common dress of the people.

Charlemagne disapproved of the fashionable outfits worn by the young bloods of the court. Alcuin of York tells the tale of the stylish courtiers, strutting about in robes of pheasant skins and peacock plumes, silks with purple ribbons and ermine robes, who were dragged off on an all-day hunt by the wily monarch. They returned home wet, bedraggled, torn by brambles and fouled by the blood of animals, only to be ordered to sleep in their clothes to dry them out and to appear the next day in the same garments "which no longer made a splendid show, being creased, shrunken and rent." Whereupon Charlemagne, "full of guile," put on his garment from the day before, an inexpensive sheepskin coat, which was still "clean, white and whole."

In Germany, when the Carolingian line failed and was replaced by the Ottonian, the Byzantine influence on courtly manners and costume was strong. The short reign of Otto II (973–83) was chiefly remarkable for his marriage to a Byzantine princess, Theophano. A practical lady, she brought scholars and artisans to Germany; fabric workers and skilled embroiderers must also have formed part of her retinue. In manuscript illustrations, Otto is shown in full Byzantine regalia wearing an ankle-length silk tunic, deeply bordered at the hem, side slit, wrist, and collar with gemmed bands of gold.

Two magnificent court robes of the period of Henry II (1002–24) are preserved in the cathedral treasury at Bamberg. These ceremonial mantles consciously imitated Mass vestments worn by the higher clergy in order to emphasize the Christian foundation of the empire. Queen Kunigunde's mantle is a huge, semicircular cape, cut from imported blue brocade. Henry's Star Mantle has an astrological motif, worked in gold and scarlet embroidery.

Several consistent trends appear in European costume from the ninth through the thirteenth centuries; first, the retention of the convenient barbarian trousers or hose for active, daily wear; second, the increasing appearance among the wealthy of elaborate styles adapted from the robes of Byzantium; third, a decided emphasis on male rather than female dress; and, finally, the spirit of mortification of the flesh and a revulsion against worldly preoccupations, inherited from the early Christian ascetics.

As costume became richer and more ostentatious, the outcries of saintly critics swelled in volume. St. Bernard of Clairvaux denounced the "pomp and pride to adorn such carrion as is your body." He continued: "People who admire themselves because of their clothes are as illogical as criminals who boast of being branded, for without the guilt of Adam, clothing would not be necessary." Occasionally the criticism had overtones of social reproach: "Think you not of the poor people that are dying of hunger and of cold? And that for a sixth part of your gay attire forty persons might be clothed, refreshed and kept from the cold?"

Court costumes of the twelfth century point up the accuracy of these complaints. While only royalty could aspire to silks and imported brocades, and then only for special occasions, the more usual woolen and linen garments of the nobility used up an inordinate amount of fabric. Men wore as an undergarment a loose shirt with either wrapped trousers or hose to cover their legs. A floor-length undertunic was next and, over that, the robe or supertunic with long, floppy sleeves that extended far over the hand. The robe was usually hitched up under the belt to display the undertunic and both garments were enriched with embroidery. A heavy, semicircular ground-length mantle completed the outfit.

Women wore a chemise, an undertunic, and a robe with tight sleeves that flared out at the wrist to a width of four feet or more. For once, men's costume seemed to draw more fire from the critics than women's styles. St. Bernard lashed out again and again: "You adorn yourself with pomp for death. Are your plumes the harness of a knight or the finery of a lady? You dress your hair like women; you catch your feet in long, wide skirts." The main objection seems to have been against the excesses of the costume, the ridiculously pointed shoes or the exaggerated trains of the robes and mantles dragging behind men of fashion.

The historical chronicles of the era, perhaps because they were written by men and generally reflect the heroic exploits of the age of chivalry, are full of lengthy descriptions of male attire. We know, for example, exactly what England's king, Richard the Lion-Hearted, wore at his wedding. He arrayed himself in a tunic of rose-colored satin, a long mantle of striped silver tissue woven with an all-over pattern of golden crescent moons, and a scarlet bonnet embroidered with gold. As historian Thomas B. Costain comments: "What the bride wore was not considered important enough to set down."

The age of the Crusades saw great advances in the design of armor. William the Conqueror had amply demonstrated in 1066 the importance of mailed cavalry. His knights wore one-piece mail suits, which looked somewhat like long johns, that apparently laced up the back. To construct these, metal wire was wrapped around a form and cut into

The bliaut, an ankle-length tunic with very full sleeves and split to the waist to be worn over chain mail (left), was widely adopted during the era of the Crusades. The shoes with long pointed toes are an example of the excesses condemned by clerics. The influence of the Levant is apparent in the garb of the statues that flank the portal of Chartres Cathedral (right). These robes were often made of silk and edged with gold braid.

open-ended circles that were then woven together, with the open ends of each link eventually flattened, drilled, and riveted together. The mail was built up gradually and shaped rather like a knitted garment.

The mail suit was worn over padded leather undergarments; it provided good protection and was flexible enough to allow free movement. It was also expensive. In the days of Charlemagne, the simple lack of a horse and armor was often the deciding factor that doomed unborn generations to a social condition of servility. In the formative years of feudalism, an armed and mounted warrior kept his freedom; the poor farmer who could not afford such luxuries sank into serfdom.

During the twelfth century, the basic chain-mail union suit developed a hood fitting closely around the head and long sleeves with mitts. Trousers or hose were made of the flexible metal, laced together

With the defeat of King Harold of England (below, center) at the Battle of Hastings and the conquest of his island kingdom by William, Duke of Normandy, Continental influence leapt the Channel. Skilled weavers followed the duke to England, where they soon developed a reputation for producing woolen goods of highest quality.

in the back and held in place with straps arranged much like a garter belt. Plate mail was introduced on a limited basis in the thirteenth century, usually to guard such vulnerable areas as the throat, knees, and elbows. Full suits of plate were not to appear on a widespread basis until the late fifteenth century. Fabric surcoats with heraldic insignia were worn over the mail to keep off the direct rays of the sun.

On a hot June day in 1215 stern knights and disgruntled barons appeared at Charter Island at Runnymede in full suits of mail and partial plate, fully armed and mounted, enduring the blazing sun as a point of pride. By the second day, most had dismounted, looking for a spot of cooling shade. On the third day of negotiations, the mail was discarded and replaced by cuirasses of tough, boiled leather, cooler and lighter than metal. And according to Costain, "on the fourth day it was

AMENTVM:FECIT: hIC hARO
L MO DVCI:

suspected that nothing in the way of armor would have been found if the rich brocaded surcoats . . . had been stripped off." One wonders what might have emerged in this military strip tease had the conference lasted a fifth day.

On the whole, the twelfth century presents a picture of a sartorial silly season. Male costume, which had incurred the wrath of the clerics, was wildly extravagant and strongly individualistic. Fabric was used almost by the mile rather than by the yard. The most significant innovation of the period appeared in mid-century when the bliaut, the overtunic worn by men, was redesigned. Formerly cut in two simple pieces, front and back, it was now cut as two separate garments, blouse and skirt, seamed together at the waist. This allowed the top to be laced close to the body while the skirts flared out with extra fullness.

Braid and broad panels of embroidery were used lavishly, almost at random, on hems, borders, sleeves, and side seams. Men wore their hair unusually long in fantastic curls and twists; beards were oiled or waxed and arranged in points, and long, wispy moustaches were cultivated. Those who could afford it wore the rich exotic fabrics that the Crusaders had come to know and love in the far-off kingdoms of Outremer—cloth of gold, silver tissue, silk, gauze, and fine damask. After generations of plain, no-nonsense homespun, European chivalry wallowed in a surfeit of fine textiles.

Oriental costume had a major impact on the styles worn by the masters of the Crusader kingdoms in the Levant. Flowing robes and turbans, cut in the Saracen fashion, were all the rage in the Christian realms of Antioch, Acre, or Jerusalem, and were eagerly adopted by the stay-at-homes in France or England. When, in 1187, the Latin kingdom of Jerusalem fell to the armies of Saladin the Great, the crusading fervor revived again in Europe and the thirteenth century was ushered in on a more sober note.

The craze for exotic and extravagant attire passed and Western costume expressed a new sense of simplicity and uniformity. Men discarded the undertunic and wore the overtunic short, belted at the waist, and cut in one piece. The sleeves were cut dolman fashion to form a deep armhole beginning almost at waist level, tapering and narrowing to fit closely at forearm and wrist. The skirts were open, front and back, from crotch to hem to permit greater freedom of movement, and were worn over hose held up at the waist by a drawstring. Decoration was modest, generally limited to embroidered bands at neck and wrist. A mantle, about the same length as the tunic, was held across the chest by a strap anchored with large, circular brooches.

In the early decades of the century, women's costume was almost identical to that of the men, with the exception that their tunics and mantles were long and swept the ground. As the century wore on, lavish decoration in the Byzantine manner began to creep back into fashion, although the basic cut of the garments remained simple. The love of rich fabrics had never died out; textiles were still imported and old costumes were handed down from one generation to another to be picked apart and carefully restyled. Fur was increasingly used, particularly for linings. Despite the preference for expensive

textiles and furs, the fashions of the period drew fewer reproaches from the clergy. The crusading spirit was still strong, though largely ineffective, and throughout Europe men and women expressed in their clothing a becoming humility and dedication to religious ideals.

By the end of the century, the crusading fervor was dead. Kings, nobles, and knights continued to raise the topic for another century or so, but nothing was actually attempted. After all was said and done, the Crusades had achieved none of their primary goals. Jerusalem and the holy places remained in Moslem hands and seemingly all that Europe had to show for decades of strife was an immense loss in money and men. There were, however, many beneficent results, although these lay in areas unforeseen by the knights of Christ: the Crusades played a major role in the decline of feudalism; towns became independent of feudal authority and urban life was born again; the Byzantine Empire, humbled by the disgraceful Fourth Crusade, gave less competition to the rising Italian merchant cities; Europe experienced an economic revolution; trade and industry revived; coined money circulated again and an elaborate system of banking sprang up almost overnight.

There were cultural gains as the Crusaders returned home with more advanced knowledge, techniques and concepts borrowed from the Byzantine and Arab worlds. As many historians have pointed out, the rediscovery of the Near East was as revolutionary in 1300 as the discovery of America was to be in 1492. Medieval man, scarcely aware of more than his own parish and county, was thrown into contact with older and richer civilizations. The medieval mind became aware that something worthwhile existed outside its own narrow scope of vision. Western Europe lost some of its provincialism and became more cosmopolitan. It was as if Europe, darkened and poorly ventilated, had suddenly thrown wide a great window opening on the rest of the world.

5

The Rebirth of Style

THE SOCIAL, POLITICAL, AND ECONOMIC UPHEAVALS that swept through Europe in the wake of the Crusades paved the way for the emergence of the Renaissance. Far more than a social or political revolution, the Renaissance was a new state of mind. For perhaps the first time in history, man viewed his recent past with contempt, dismissing the Middle Ages, somewhat unfairly, as a hopelessly backward period.

For his basic cultural orientation, Renaissance man looked back to classical antiquity and attempted to create a way of life based on the glories of ancient Greece and the grandeur of ancient Rome. Italy, the birthplace of the Renaissance, had an advantage unshared by the rest of Europe, for the classical civilization of ancient Italy had never been entirely extinguished but lay close to the surface, waiting to be reawakened. Yet Renaissance classicism went far beyond simple reconstruction of the classic past; in many ways the new and exuberant culture of the Renaissance bore as little resemblance to classical antiquity as it did to the discredited Middle Ages.

Renaissance society was essentially urban, its roots deep in town life. The competitive commercial activities of the Italian city-states and the fluid social mobility of the middle class had contributed increasingly to the development of secularism, that is, open concern with this world and the unabashed pursuit of its pleasures and delights—including, of course, the wearing of magnificent clothing. This represented a sharp break with the medieval tendency to emphasize the eternal bliss of the hereafter while condemning as a waste of time or sinful any preoccupation with the illusory goods of this transitory existence.

Out of secularism developed individualism, emphasing the uniqueness of every man, free to realize his highest potentialities rather than remaining another anonymous cog in the cosmic wheel. The Middle Ages had tended to restrict the individual to his inherited station in life, providing security at the cost of individual achievement. By contrast, the Renaissance glorified the talented, versatile individual capable of attaining excellence in many fields. This was the Universal Man, who could with equal competence lead an army, improvise a sonnet, translate Latin epigrams, play and compose for the lute, converse in several languages, excel in athletic contests, and, if need be, govern a principality. Those who could do such things had a quality called *virtù*, a combination of extraordinary ability, talent, and dynamism.

No European monarch so perfectly embodied the spirit of the High Renaissance as Francis 1, whose court was graced by the presence of Leonardo da Vinci, the very epitome of the Universal Man, and whose reign was marked by the full flowering of the Renaissance in France. In Jean Clouet's portrait opposite, Francis wears a doublet of heavy brocade under a loose Venetian gown characterized by wide, turned-back sleeves fastened at the shoulders. The French king also favored soft, full caps, often trimmed with feathers or fur.

The leading city of Italy was Florence, which owed its cultural supremacy to the brilliance of its creative geniuses—Dante, Giotto, Boccaccio, Petrarch—and its affluence to the commercial acuity of its citizens. Great banking houses flourished, and by the fourteenth century the major financial transactions of all Europe were conducted there.

The textile industry formed a vital part of the Florentine economy. Although wool itself was not produced in Tuscany, the Florentine craftsmen knew secret and highly advanced techniques whereby unbleached or raw wool imported from Flanders or England could be scoured, dyed, and given a special finish. The fabrics were then exported back to northern Europe, where they were much preferred to the local products. The most important of the Florentine guilds, the Calimala, handled only the dyeing and finishing of fine woven cloth. A slightly lesser guild, the Arte della Lana, covered all aspects of manufacture from raw wool to finished cloth. A third guild, the Arte della Seta, wove and processed silk into the beautiful brocades, damasks, satins, taffetas, velvets, and tissues of gold and silver so highly prized by the wealthy and the aristocratic.

Other cities of northern Italy, Lucca for example, also supported flourishing textile industries. Spain, Flanders, and France produced wools and fine linens; in northern Europe the Hanseatic League controlled an active trade in furs. Rare silks and tapestry weaves were still

The Renaissance, which affected every aspect of life in Western Europe, brought with it the first major change in costume in two centuries, as both sexes abandoned the flowing robes of the Middle Ages. A heightened interest in fashion gave employ to countless local artisans, whose tiny shops (right) turned out clothes and accessories for an increasingly affluent and style-conscious market. The Florentine wool guild, whose symbol was a fleecy lamb (above), gained international renown, as did the pointed shoes (left) produced by Spanish cobblers.

imported from the Near East, India, and China, but it was the prodigious activity of European textile centers and the availability of locally made and less expensive luxury goods that inspired the rapid innovations in costume that characterize the Renaissance.

The care and cleaning of the fabulous textiles was a major concern of the Renaissance housewife, who boiled linens and scrubbed wools in tepid or cold water with homemade lye soap. Some silk could be washed, but luxury fabrics generally required special attention. Fuller's earth moistened with lye was rubbed on grease spots, or the garment might be put to soak overnight in warm white wine or vinegar. Garments were sometimes turned when they became hopelessly stained; that is, they were taken apart and resewn inside out. Fine textiles were recut and restyled for as long as the material held together. Children's garments were commonly fashioned from cast-off adult clothing. When gold or silver tissues or brocades reached the point of no return, they were burned to recover the precious metal.

Even princely households were careful not to waste fine fabrics. An expensive robe listed in the dowry of a bride often reappears years later in the lady's will. Furs usually required professional attention, but for home care they were brushed with fine oils. Vermin were a constant problem; most households were crawling with fleas, lice, and bedbugs. Garments were stored in chests or presses of cypress wood with layers

The fitted clothes associated
with the High Renaissance
gained acceptance with men
more readily than with women,
who were slow to abandon the
voluminous, deep-sleeved tunics
(left) of an earlier age. The
most characteristic garment of
the period was a belted gown
known as the houppelande
(right), which was always generous in its use of fabric and
often extravagant in its detailing.

of bay leaves or aromatic pine needles. A standard wardrobe item was
the flea coat, a shaggy lounging robe, often of wolfskin, whose purpose
was to induce the fleas to leave the wearer and dive into the fur. By the
sixteenth century it had shrunk to a mere flea fur, the hide of a small
animal elegantly mounted in gold and gems and carried in the hand or
draped around the arm like a stole.

During the first half of the fourteenth century costume changed
little from the styles of the previous era. The secular costume shown in
Giotto's frescoes still features the plain tunic with deep dolman sleeves,
often worn under a cyclas, or sleeveless overtunic. Workingmen wore
the tunic just below the knee, older men wore it to the ankle, and
women's tunics dragged the ground. The colors were clear but muted,
and decorative bands of gold embroidery were applied sparingly and
with taste. Then, in mid-century, men abruptly abandoned the long
gown in favor of a short, fitted jacket and long, tight hose. The origin
of this new style cannot be fixed with any accuracy. But although the
homeland of the new style cannot be identified, its beginnings can be
traced to contemporary developments in arms and armor.

Chain mail, which gave little protection against the new and powerful crossbows and the even newer crude firearms, was gradually being
replaced by plate. Chain mail was still used in areas requiring flexibility,
but solid plate afforded more security. Plate mail was cut and hinged to
fit closely to the body. The thigh coverings, or cuisses, did away with
the need for the long skirts of the old chain tunic. The short, virile
lines of the military look were then taken over into civilian costume.

The short jacket of the early Renaissance had many names and many local styles. The cotehardie had long, closefitting sleeves buttoned from elbow to wrist. Cut very tightly to the body, it reached to the upper thigh and usually buttoned down the front. A heavy ornamented belt was worn slung just over the hip bones. The pourpoint was similar in cut except for the sleeves, which were cleverly tailored to allow free movement of the arms. It was usually heavier than the cotehardie, often made of several layers of fabric quilted together. The new short look exposed well-turned masculine legs, now covered with skintight hose, cut on the bias to get the snuggest possible fit. Each leg was cut separately and fastened to the inside of the jacket with points, that is, corded laces somewhat like shoestrings. An impressively heraldic effect was often achieved through the use of two contrasting fabrics, the left leg and left arm matching the right side of the jacket, the right leg and arm matching the left side.

This new look delighted the young and, not unpredictably, scandalized the old. All over Europe the conservative critics tuned up again, inveighing against the "horrible disordinate scantiness of clothing that through its shortness does not cover the shameful members of man. . . . When the wearer stoops over he reveals his breeks and what is inside. . . . These garments are so tight that help is essential both for dressing and undressing and when they are taken off it looks like skinning."

The problem was that the hose were two separate articles, and although they were supposed to overlap decently at the top, there must have been numerous sins of omission. Blue laws failed to help. An English edict attempted to restrict this usage to the upper classes by decreeing that "nobody below the rank of gentleman may wear a coat so short that when he stands erect it fails to cover his buttocks." Culprits were fined twenty shillings, a hefty sum for those days. Finally, around 1370, a man of genius came up with the notion of sewing the two pieces together at the rear, leaving an opening in front, which was then covered by a separate triangle of cloth called the braye. This modest addition eventually burst into full and glorious flower as the codpiece.

Conservatives and clerics were not the only men to lament the passing of the old long gowns; tailors and cloth merchants were in utter despair. The new styles were ruining them. But just when the sky of fashion seemed darkest, a new outer garment appeared that required enough material to have made two of the old surcoats. This was the houppelande, a very wide gown, belted high at the waist with extremely full, flaring sleeves. It was often lined with fur, decorated with cutwork and elaborately dagged; that is, the hem and sleeve edges were cut in intricately scalloped or leaf-shaped patterns. The long houppelande went out of style around 1425, but a shorter version remained in vogue for another twenty-five years or so. The headdress worn with this robe also required an inordinate amount of fabric; it was essentially a hood with an extremely elongated peak, nine feet or more in length, which was wound around the head like a turban, then draped across the chest and hung down the back.

Women's costumes were no less elegant and extravagant. All through the fourteenth century and well into the fifteenth, women

Overleaf: Pages in quilted and padded doublets, noblemen in floor-sweeping houppelandes, and ladies of the court in figure-flattering gowns and wired butterfly headdresses—in short, a sight to warm the cockles of a Renaissance tailor's heart.

71

wore two basic garments, the cotehardie and the sideless gown. A long mantle was added for outerwear or for state occasions. The women's cotehardie was a long gown fitted snugly to the body as far as the hips, where it flared out into a circle. It buttoned or laced down the front; its tight sleeves were buttoned from the wrist to well above the elbow. If worn alone the sleeves were usually elbow length with long, hanging streamers; the richly decorated sleeves of the underrobe covered the forearms. The sideless gown, or surcoat, barely hung on the shoulders; the armholes were cut away in deep curves reaching well below the hip bone to display the undergown and the jeweled girdle. The surcoat was usually lined throughout with fur and ornamented down the front with jeweled buttons or studs. This enchanting and essentially modest costume nonetheless came in for its share of criticism; the cutouts of the surcoat were referred to as "hell's windows." But it was a popular style, and variations of it remained in fashion for about two centuries.

The most significant fashion trends of the fifteenth century originated in Italy and were picked up, with local variations, by the courts and cities of northern Europe. While Italian costume was by no means standardized and often varied radically from one city-state to another, a fairly consistent pattern can be noted. The short houppelande was introduced early in the century and worn well into the 1440's. By mid-century it had all but disappeared and was replaced by a short jacket, known variously as the pourpoint, courtepy, or doublet.

Previously the pourpoint had been worn primarily as an undergarment to provide anchorage for the hose. Now it was worn as an outer garment and took the form of a tight, closefitting jacket with sleeves puffed and padded to the elbow and buttoned snugly over the forearm. For variation, a tight, sleeveless jacket or a short, open-sided surcoat

might be worn over it. The shoulder line was broad and virile, accentuated by puffed sleeves. As the skirts of the jacket continued to shrink, interest was focused on the upper part of the body. By the end of the century, the jacket had become a proper doublet; it fell to the waist and had a low neck, which exposed the shirt, a standard undergarment of the past now emerging into the light of day. Long gowns were still worn by older men or for formal occasions.

Women's costumes incorporated many features originated by men. The women's houppelandes were almost identical to those worn by their husbands and brothers, but with even longer sleeves and trains. Rich fabrics were preferred, heavily embroidered with flowers, leaves, fruits, scrolls, and heraldic motifs. The very wealthy had professionals enrich their decorations with gold thread, pearls, and other gems. Women of modest means bought plain cloth and embroidered it.

By mid-century the houppelande had shed much of its excess yardage and had taken the form of a simple, high-waisted dress, still having a train but with closefitting sleeves. Toward the end of the century the train disappeared, the waist remained high, and the sleeves were cut separately and tied to the armholes with points. An outer gown, unfitted and entirely open down the sides, was occasionally worn over the basic dress. Italian women generally favored a round turban, or their own hair elaborately dressed and covered with a sheer veil. They never went in for the eccentric headgear worn in northern Europe.

By and large, Italian costume of the fifteenth century was simple and dignified. Perhaps because Italian society was dominated by sober upper-middle-class bankers and merchants rather than by feudal lords, fashion never developed any of the absurd excesses that were all the rage in Burgundy, France, Flanders, and England. The period is well

The fifteenth-century dukes of Burgundy were known throughout Europe for their enormous wealth and their fanatical dedication to fashion. The court of Philip the Good, dressed all in cream (left) for a falcon hunt, set styles in dress for all of Western Europe. The period is remembered for the sheer multiplicity of styles it generated— and for a particular detail, the organ-pipe pleats seen at right, that are the signature of the age.

documented in Italian Renaissance art, and with few exceptions the secular costumes illustrated are characterized by exquisite proportions and almost classical simplicity. The decoration, although rich, is tastefully restrained. The flamboyant styles observed by Pisanello were almost certainly special confections for carnivals and costume balls. In the art of fashion, as in the arts of painting, sculpture, and architecture, the Italians strove for a formal beauty based on elegance and harmony.

The fashion scene was far different in northern Europe, particularly at the court of the duke of Burgundy, whose love of splendid exhibitionism was equaled only by his fabulous wealth. Philip the Bold apparently initiated this trend in the late fourteenth century. For a great feast at Amiens he appeared in a voluminous black-velvet houppelande, the left sleeve of which was decorated with roses worked in gold, sapphires, rubies, and pearls. During the course of the banquet he laid this aside to display a coat of red velvet with embroidered polar bears in jeweled gold collars. Philip's successors—John the Fearless, Philip the Good, and Charles the Bold—inherited his mania for sartorial splendor and throughout the fifteenth century Burgundian costume went from one extreme to another. The duchy was so wealthy that Burgundian styles influenced almost all of northern Europe; sleeves were wider, gowns longer, doublets shorter, and headgear more ostentatious.

Women wore long-trained gowns fully lined with fur, high-waisted with extreme décolletage, and topped off with elaborate headdresses. The horned or heart-shaped head covering was popular throughout the first half of the fifteenth century, although—as one writer commented —it often made the wearer look like a tipsy cow. Hair, both real and false, covered with a gold net was piled up at either side of the head to support these elegant monstrosities. Foreheads were shaved to give a fashionably high hairline. When the steeple-shaped hennin was introduced at mid-century, not a trace of hair was allowed to show. The steeple hats were usually topped with a long gauze veil, or with elaborately starched and folded sheer linen, artfully arranged over wire. The effect was fantastic, ridiculous, and often curiously attractive.

Women of the middle class made do with plain linen, starched, folded, and creased into eccentric shapes. Variations of these court headdresses, taken up by the peasantry, have remained a part of national folk costume in many parts of Europe until the present century. The middle class, even the wealthy upper middle class of bankers and merchants, seldom allowed itself the extremes of fashion indulged in by the aristocracy. Even when its choice was not restricted by sumptuary laws, which was often the case, the upper bourgeoisie was reluctant to adopt the excesses of the nobility.

Sumptuary laws, which regulated extravagance in dress on ostensibly moral or religious grounds, had been around since at least Roman times, when the Senate had vainly tried to curb the rage for silk. Adam Smith was later to describe such laws as "the highest impertinence and presumption in kings and ministers." Philip the Fair of France published in the thirteenth century a series of edicts restricting furs and luxury fabrics to the nobility, even going so far as to specify which qualities of cloth could be worn by the different social classes. The Renaissance saw dozens of these restrictive laws solemnly passed in every major European city. Sometimes the laws were aimed at banning certain elements of fashion altogether; low necklines, trains, and pointed shoes, for example, were outlawed in Milan and Venice. In other areas the laws limited the number of silk and velvet garments that could be owned at one time by a single individual. Furs were portioned out according to rank: ermine for royalty, humble squirrel or rabbit for the bourgeoisie. Of course, the real function of these laws was to confine extremes of fashion to the nobility to preserve class distinctions.

The increasing wealth and social mobility of the middle class had steadily gnawed away at the foundations of the aristocracy. By the late fifteenth century the real wealth of Europe was in the hands of the bankers and merchants, who were as a result also beginning to control the power structure. The nobility still had their titles, the outward show of power, and their pedigrees, but in actual fact feudalism was dead. Only through sumptuary laws could the aristocrats maintain the illusion of their supremacy by legislating visible differences between themselves and the bourgeoisie they so despised and feared.

Toward the end of the fifteenth century it was apparent that a new political ideal was spreading through Europe. Feudalism was done for. The pomp and glory still remained—many of its economic and social traditions were to survive into the eighteenth century—but the actual authority was gone, taken over by a new political structure, the centralized monarchy. Spain was unified through the marriage of Ferdinand II of Aragon to Isabella of Castile and León; the Moors were defeated and driven out; and the feudal aristocracy, now reduced to mere court ornamentation, was forced to look to the new lands beyond the sea as an outlet for its ambitions.

In Germany, the imperial title had become almost the birthright of the House of Habsburg, which under Maximilian I (Holy Roman emperor 1493–1519) became the most powerful family in all Europe.

To achieve the high theater that was international Gothic fashion, women wore dresses with abundant trains, deep décolletage, and considerable padding. They also plucked their eyebrows and shaved their foreheads for dramatic effect, as the Franco-Flemish portrait at near right indicates. These elaborate coiffeurs were frequently encased in a sheer fabric headcloth supported by a wire framework (far right), the effect of which was frequently both arresting and very feminine.

Maximilian, so to speak, believed in making love, not war. He himself married the sole heiress of Charles the Bold of Burgundy, and their numerous children were betrothed to half the princely courts of Europe, including Spain, where Philip the Fair was wed to the unbalanced daughter of Isabella. Their son Charles was to become the most powerful ruler of his time, king of Spain and Holy Roman emperor.

England was beginning to emerge as a major power. Shortly after the Hundred Years' War ended in 1453, the country was torn by the Wars of the Roses, an essentially feudal power struggle between the houses of York and Lancaster. However, the death of the last Yorkist king left the throne vacant for the upstart Henry Tudor, who centralized authority by creating a new nobility directly dependent on his patronage. France, too, had been badly shaken by the Hundred Years' War, but under Louis XI the country was transformed from a feudal kingdom into a modern state. The duchy of Burgundy was annexed and the duchy of Brittany safely gathered into the French fold.

It was inevitable that European attention should be drawn to the rich and divided land of Italy, which so conspicuously lacked a strong centralized government. France invaded in 1494 and again in 1498. When Spain interfered, Italy was turned into a battleground where European powers vied for supremacy. The invasion of Francis I in 1515 again disturbed the balance of power, and in 1527 the imperial troops of Charles V viciously sacked Rome, subjugated most of Italy, and terminated the High Renaissance.

Sixteenth-century costume reflected the new concept of nationalism. Specific styles were associated with specific countries. Writers speak of a French hood, a Spanish farthingale, an Italian gown, or a

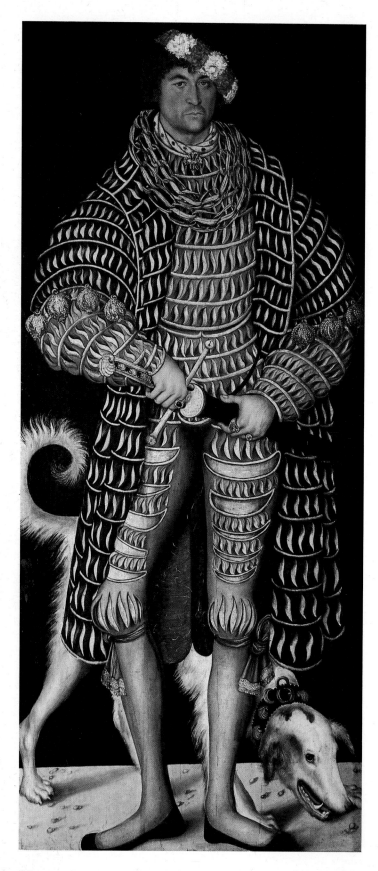

One of the most singular developments in High Renaissance fashion was slashing, a technique that permitted the wearer to display several layers of splendid fabric simultaneously. Like most styles of the period, slashing was initially treated with some restraint (below)—and eventually carried to ridiculous extremes, particularly in Germany, as evidenced by the portrait of Henry, Duke of Saxony, at left. Both costumes feature codpieces.

German cap. The French invaders took the culture and costumes of the Italian Renaissance back across the Alps with them. Italian styles developed in the last decades of the fifteenth century provided the basic garments that were later adapted and modified throughout Europe. For women, the typical gown was made up of a tight, square-necked bodice with full, flowing sleeves, which were usually folded back to expose the lining. The waistline was high early in the century, but later under French and Spanish influence it dropped to a sharp point low on the abdomen. Skirts supported by farthingales ballooned out until they seemed to hang from the rim of a cartwheel somehow supported around the waist. Basic men's wear consisted of a doublet, usually low cut to reveal the shirt; the hose, which were still attached to the doublet; and a cloak or cape, which varied considerably from one region to another. The long robe for men was seldom worn except for state occasions. From this modest beginning, the pacesetters of the sixteenth century were to evolve unusually distinctive national styles.

One of the strangest aspects of High Renaissance style was the practice of slashing. According to historians, it originated in 1477, when Charles the Bold was slain in battle. The victorious Swiss and their German mercenaries looted the tents of the Burgundians and patched their own ragged garments with odd bits and pieces of fine textiles. Somehow this flashy new look caught on, and by the early 1500's slashing was used throughout Europe. It consisted of cutting slashes in the outer costume and pulling the inner garments or the lining out through the slits. The practice was most extreme in Germany where garments were slashed in a bewildering fashion, each leg or arm cut in a different pattern. Slashing was also sometimes used in women's clothing.

Another innovation of the period was the division of hose into two separate garments. The upper portion was known as upper stocks, slops, trunk hose, or breeches; the lower portion was called nether stocks or lower hose. Often the parts were sewn together for greater ease in dressing. Early in the sixteenth century the trunk hose reached just below the knee, but by mid-century they had crawled up the leg to about the middle of the thigh, where they were heavily padded and slashed. The modest braye of the previous century developed into the full-blown codpiece, one of the most curious elements ever seen in Western male costume.

Although usually cut from the same material as the trunk hose or breeches, the codpiece was a separate item, laced to the hose and the doublet with points. Codpieces were heavily boned and padded to jut out aggressively between the breeches and the skirts of the vest, giving the impression of an advanced state of satyriasis. Predictably, conservatives were shocked. But in defiance of criticism the codpiece continued to protrude triumphantly until around 1580, when it suddenly deflated and disappeared altogether.

By mid-century the Italian influence in costume was replaced by the severe and formal fashions of Spain. Under Charles V and his successor Philip II, Spain was the most powerful state in Europe, due largely to the rich commercial cities of the Spanish Netherlands and the seemingly inexhaustible wealth of the New World. Spanish etiquette was

rigid and unbending, and Spanish costume was no less so, designed to rise above the frailties of the flesh and the weaknesses of human nature. The old deep, square neckline of the doublet gradually filled in to become a high, tightly fastened collar. The body of the doublet was whaleboned and bombasted, bulging out at the waist or abdomen to form the peasecod belly.

Women wore the farthingale, a petticoat supported by a framework of graduated cane or metal hoops to allow the skirts to fall in a stiff cone. Women's bodices were also boned, and heavy corsets known as "Spanish bodies" compressed the torso into a smaller but equally geometric cone. Only undergarments were of soft, delicate materials. Skirts, bodices, doublets, breeches, capes, and mantles were cut from heavy fabrics—brocades, velvets, satins, and taffetas. Somber colors were the rule. Black in particular became the hallmark of Spanish style. Decoration was rich and resplendent, gold braid being used lavishly.

The court of England, the only country successfully to oppose Spain, furnishes excellent examples of the varieties of fashion of this era. The century opened modestly enough under the parsimonious Henry VII, notorious for his lack of interest in fine clothing. The Franco-Burgundian styles of the previous century were still being worn. Doublets reached below the knees, and fur-lined robes swept the ground. Women wore a simple gown, tightly fitted to the upper body, with bell-shaped sleeves. The gable or "dog kennel" headdress was the most distinctive article of feminine attire. It consisted of a stiffened coif with a band of jeweled metal framing the face, and an embroidered hood that fell down in back to hide the hair.

When Henry VIII inherited the throne, he set about spending the money his father had so carefully hoarded. New fashions appeared almost overnight. Elements of French, Spanish, and German style appeared and disappeared, rapidly reflecting the king's foreign—or matrimonial—policies. Henry's first wife, Catherine of Aragon, is generally credited with the introduction of the Spanish farthingale. As worn by this unfortunate lady, the farthingale was a hooped petticoat of fairly modest dimensions, combined with a tight busk that came just below the breasts. Her gowns were essentially the same as the previous fashion, bell-sleeved and square-necked, with a normal waistline, but now the skirts were split down the center front to display the ornate

brocades of the petticoat. Undersleeves matching the petticoat were cut separately and attached to the underbodice. The sleeves of the gown were turned back almost to the shoulders to reveal the fur lining.

Catherine also brought to England the Spanish cloak, a long, stiff fur-lined cape slit at the side front for armholes. Her portraits show her wearing the early Tudor gable headdress. Before her marriage to Henry, Catherine was once reduced to only two dresses, both much the worse for wear, for both her father and her father-in-law were unusually stingy men. By contrast, Henry VIII dressed his bride resplendently, and for about twenty years she received all the honor and affection that her essentially selfish spouse had to offer. But she could not give him a son; therefore, spurred by his "tender conscience" and the bewitching dark eyes of Anne Boleyn, Henry set Catherine aside and took Anne as a bride.

Anne had spent a great deal of time in France, where Henry's sister Mary Tudor had briefly served as queen to the aged Louis XII. Naturally, she favored French styles, which at that time were among the most elegant in Europe. Anne's major contribution to court dress was the French hood, a neatly rounded little cap set far back on the head. French gowns, which also appeared in England at this time, differed from the English styles in that gown and petticoat were usually cut from the same fabric and the sleeves slashed to expose the delicate silk undergarment. But Anne also failed to give Henry a male heir. Even the king could not bear the thought of another messy divorce with half of Europe sniggering behind his back. Anne was therefore charged with multiple adulteries and incest and was beheaded.

Wife number three, Jane Seymour, was around barely long enough to have her portrait painted and to bear Henry a son. By this time, both French and Spanish styles were anathema at the English court. Jane's "English" gowns have big turned-back sleeves with slashing confined to the undersleeves. Perhaps to emphasize her own purely English ancestry, Jane went back to the gable hood, now smaller and neater in shape. She died giving Henry his son, and the lusty monarch was once again on the marriage market.

In his youth Henry had been a splendid, handsome man with the constitution of an ox, but at age forty-six he was beginning to feel his years Grossly overweight, he suffered from gout, ulcerated veins, and a slight dose of syphilis. His armor, preserved in the Tower of London, indicates that he was a powerful male animal. One suit for sword fighting on foot is composed of 235 separate pieces of plate weighing ninety-four pounds. In it the king stood six feet three inches tall and measured forty-five inches around the chest, thirty-eight around the waist. Another suit, made at about the time of his fourth venture into matrimony, had a chest of fifty-eight inches and a waist of fifty-four.

Henry had begun to adopt the grossly overpadded styles popularized in Germany, apparently because the huge puffed sleeves added bulk through the shoulders and minimized the royal paunch. His costumes were usually color co-ordinated, harmonizing shades of red, green, cream, or yellow played off against the dark, soft fur lining of the robe. Perhaps as an anti-Spanish gesture, he seldom wore black. The

Germanic cut of Henry's costumes echoes the styles favored by his fourth wife, Anne of Cleves. She was a political bride; through her, Henry hoped to gain the support of the German princes in his struggle against Charles V. But the alliance fell through; Charles and Henry were politically reconciled, and poor Anne was superfluous. Worried, not unduly, about the possibility of losing her head, Anne fainted in joyous shock when it turned out that all her husband wanted was a divorce. She received the title of the "king's sister," and an excellent settlement. She continued to enjoy court life, turning up in a new gown on every possible occasion, and remained on amiable terms with her "brother" and the two young princesses, Mary and Elizabeth.

Henry married twice more: first, Catherine Howard who, like her cousin Anne Boleyn, was beheaded; finally Catherine Parr, who survived the royal Bluebeard. These last two queens apparently made few changes in basic fashion; Catherine Howard went back to the French hood during her short term and Catherine Parr introduced a flat Germanic cap similar to those worn by men.

During the short reign of Edward VI (1547–53) much of the extreme fullness disappeared from male costume, and the vest or jerkin became shorter to expose more of the trunk hose or breeches. At first glance, there would appear to be little or no change in women's fashions, but three almost insignificant changes indicate the shape of things to come. First, the deep, square neckline was totally filled in with fabric, usually matching the sleeve lining, which folded back at the neck to show the ruffled and gathered chemise rising suddenly right up to the ears. Secondly, the bodice was much stiffer; the Spanish body or corset was now almost universally worn. Finally, the waistline was lower, moving toward a deep point in front. These trends continued through the reign of Mary and became even more severe and formal. Mary's political policy was pro-Spanish, as her mother, of course, was Catherine of Aragon, and she herself was wedded to Philip of Spain, son and heir of Charles V. At about this time there appeared in England the Spanish surcoat, a long, heavy robe with leg-of-mutton or short, puffed sleeves, usually worn open down the front, but occasionally buttoned or fastened as far as the waist. Spanish influence remained strong during Mary's lifetime.

The real fun began with the accession of Elizabeth I (1558–1603), who inherited her father's love of luxury as well as his political acumen and iron will. The cone-shaped farthingale became even stiffer and wider at the bottom, and the French wheel-shaped farthingale was imported to keep it company. In the French style the bodice was extremely narrow and came to a point very low in front. The circular framework shot straight out from the hips and the skirt fell over the outer rim to drop in a vertical line to the ground. This outlandish contraption was, of course, for court costume only. Common women wore a large sausagelike pad, bluntly called the bum roll, which was tied around the waist under the skirts. The effect of these stiff hoops was to totally geometrize the body and to provide an unbending framework to display the almost vulgarly ornate and overdecorated fabrics that characterize the Elizabethan era.

The ruff which Catherine de Médicis introduced to France on her marriage to Henry II in 1533 reached England during the early years of Elizabeth's reign. Developed from the modest lace and flutings that earlier had decorated the neckline of the shirt or chemise, the ruff rose out of the high collar of the doublet. By the 1570's, it was a separate item of apparel, basically formed of a long band of fine linen or lace, heavily starched and gathered on the inner edge to a neckband. The ruff was worn by both men and women, and its size was in direct proportion to the status of the wearer. Unfortunately, it covered the bosom, which Elizabeth, as a virgin queen, was entitled to expose. The so-called "Elizabethan compromise" resolved the dilemma: the ruff was opened in front and supported in back by huge, gauzy wings held up by wire. Elizabeth was proud of her tiny feet as well as her alabaster bosom; from about the 1580's on skirts were shortened to just above the ankles to show off her delicate feet in fantastically gemmed high-heeled shoes.

Male costume from the 1580's on was particularly attractive. The Spanish influence, still supreme on the Continent, gave way in England to a more graceful and light-hearted style. As the queen got older, her courtly swains got younger and dressed in bright colors and novelty fabrics. The doublet, still with the heavily bombasted peasecod belly, fit very snugly to the torso, and the trunk hose—usually called pansid slops—barely covered the buttocks to call attention to a marvelous great length of leg. The nether hose fitted like a second skin. They were now knitted, sometimes of silk, rather than being bias cut from light wool, and they were often embellished with embroidered clocks or sprigs of flowers.

Costume was a serious art at the court of Elizabeth. State robes are not, of course, to be taken as typical female dress of the period. Ladies of the nobility and upper middle class wore dresses cut to the same general pattern, but were careful not to outshine their royal mistress. At Elizabeth's death her wardrobe was immense, numbering hundreds of pairs of tiny, narrow shoes and thousands of dresses that were no doubt picked over gleefully by her successor, James I of England and VI of Scotland, and his queen, Anne of Denmark. James, however, did not maintain the sartorial splendor of the court: "He would never change his clothes, till very ragged and he never washed his hands," commented a historian, who added: "He had a very brave queen."

English court costume never succeeded on the Continent, where high fashion was based on French and Spanish modes. Indeed, Europeans generally considered English costume rather grotesque and ridiculous, although the prevailing Spanish trend was no less so. In the seventeenth century Spanish styles were to become quite outrageous and rather old-fashioned as the grandees and their ladies piously preserved many of the eccentricities of the great age of Philip II. But Spain had had its day and was soon to decline into a state of formal and shabby gentility. Under a strong king, Henry IV, and his successors, France, which had verged on political disaster during the regency of Catherine de Médicis and the reigns of her ineffectual sons, was now ready to assume the role of arbiter of elegance for all Europe.

England's Virgin Queen had a particular fondness for handsome men, and her entourage always included a number of exquisitely dressed young courtiers such as the one seen above. It is thought that the subject of this Hilliard portrait may be Robert Devereux, an impetuous youth who was the aging queen's favorite until his plotting against her forced Elizabeth to have the headstrong earl executed.

6

Elegance and Excess

The seventeenth century was marked by unremitting political and social turbulence in Europe. Costume reflected this turmoil with readily recognizable national elements superimposed on a basically international style. In the self-portrait opposite, Flemish painter Peter Paul Rubens and his wife, Isabella, are shown dressed in the rich but casual elegance favored by the wealthy upper middle class. Isabella's rounded stomacher · is Netherlandish in style but she wears a distinctively Spanish ruff. Her tall felt hat is extremely up-to-date and rather rare for this period. The painter's soft, falling collar is also quite fashionable and somewhat ahead of its time.

THE SIXTEENTH CENTURY, which had opened so auspiciously for France, ended in a long period of bitterness and disillusionment during which the country was torn by religious and civil wars. Early in the century, Francis I had won international prestige for himself and his country by the conquest of Milan. A virile, brilliant figure and a true Renaissance prince, Francis I attracted artists, architects, poets, and humanists from Italy to the French court. His ambassadors and diplomats invested heavily in masterpieces of Italian and antique art; French artists were subsidized to study in Italy; and elegant châteaux sprang up almost overnight throughout the Loire valley. Unfortunately, in political and military matters Francis' talents were mediocre. Totally outclassed by the forces of Charles V, his army was all but annihilated in 1525 at the Battle of Pavia; Francis was taken prisoner, and Charles V became master of Italy.

Francis was maneuvered into a political marriage with Charles's sister; he was later quoted to the effect that he would have married the emperor's mule to escape Spanish protective custody. He returned to France sadder but not much wiser. To gain the support of the papacy he accepted Pope Clement VII's young ward, Catherine de Médicis, as a bride for his son Henry. The French nobility saw the marriage as a mésalliance and never forgave Catherine her middle-class background.

Neglected by her husband and outshone by his mistress, the bewitching Diane de Poitiers, Catherine was none the less influential in bringing Italian culture, cuisine, and fashion into the French court. She fulfilled her primary duty by producing seven children, but it was rather a mixed blessing, since both she and her young husband suffered from congenital syphilis, a grim legacy they passed on to their offspring. In 1559 Henry II was killed in a freak tournament accident, and Catherine assumed the regency in the name of her eldest son. For the next thirty years she controlled the declining fortunes of France. Her sons—Francis II, Charles IX, and Henry III—were weak, lacking in authority, and generally uninterested in government.

Although in other respects Henry III's reign was one of the low points in French political history, his passion for costume resulted in positive benefits for the country's textile industry, which he supported and encouraged. Both Tours and Lyon became famous for silk manufacture, and the silkworm itself was cultivated with moderate success.

By the end of the century new silk factories had opened at Nîmes, Orléans, and Montpellier, and silk stockings were knitted in the mills of Dourdan. Since sumptuary laws restricted and severely taxed imported textiles, the court and upper bourgeoisie followed the royal example and draped themselves lavishly in French silks and brocades.

At the court of Henry III fashions were refined and effeminate. His epicene courtiers and favorites assimilated elements from Italian, Spanish, German, Polish, and Hungarian fashions. The king himself was particularly fascinated by female costume. On one occasion he attended a ball dressed in full farthingale and low-cut bodice, with yards of pearls draped around his neck. Even more astonishing was a costume described by the Duke of Sully: "I shall never forget the fantastic and extravagant equipage and attitude in which I found this prince in his cabinet. He had a sword at his side, a Spanish hood hung down upon his shoulders, a little cap such as collegians wear, upon his head, and a basket of little dogs hung to a broad ribbon about his neck."

Henry was said to have been late to both his coronation and wedding because of last-minute fussing with his ruff, but he was on time for his assassination: he was struck down by a fanatical monk determined to free his country from this "Prince of Sodom with his court of silks and blood." The crown passed to Henry of Navarre, of a collateral branch of the royal house, and France began to emerge from its long ordeal.

Under Henry IV, a man of simple tastes and good sense, France recovered some of its lost prestige. Reared as a Calvinist, Henry realized that the French would never accept a Protestant king. He accordingly converted to Catholicism, cheerfully remarking that "Paris is worth a Mass." At the same time he resolved the country's religious problems by extending religious toleration and civil liberties to Protestants. Like Henry II, he married into Italian wealth. His queen was Marie de Médicis, niece and heiress of the Grand Duke of Tuscany. Court wits referred to Marie as the "fat banker;" upon the king's assassination in 1610, she acted as regent for the young Louis XIII.

The fashions of the early decades of the seventeenth century followed the styles of the previous era, but with a new sense of sobriety and decorum. The lavish use of jeweled fabrics began to decline except for the most formal court costume. Gem incrustation gave way to ribbons, buttons, lace, and bows. The peasecod belly on men's doublets grew smaller. The enormous balloon sleeves also shrank, giving the arm a more normal outline. Slashing, though still practiced, was more restrained. Men still wore hose and breeches with long nether hose, but thick padding and bombasting was less common than it had been. Usually the heavy fabric and interlining provided enough weight and stiffness for the garments to hold their shape. While the ruff was still popular, it was gradually being replaced by the whisk, a flat lace collar supported on a wire frame.

Henry IV himself paid little attention to fashion and even made a point of dressing modestly. Addressing the Parlement of Paris, he said: "I have come to speak to you not in royal robes or with sword and cape like my predecessors, but dressed like the father of a family in a doublet." Venetian ambassadors were shocked to see the king leaving

Catherine de Médicis, blessed with a superabundance of personal dynamism, was cursed with four weak sons, three of whom became kings of France. The last of these was Henry III, a sometime transvestite whose devotion to flamboyant costume was shared by a host of effete courtiers (above).

his apartments with his doublet half unbuttoned, his breeches drooping, and his points undone, allowing his hose to fall untidily around his shoetops. Like most men of his time, he was not unduly clean; "Don't wash," he once wrote to a mistress; "I'm coming over after lunch."

Women's costumes also showed gradual modifications. Dresses were still cut with separate skirt and bodice, a style commonly followed since the 1570's. Bodices were tightly fitted over corsets designed to obliterate the natural lines of the body. Corsets were usually made of strong silk, linen, or lightweight leather, solidly lined with strips of whalebone—a broad busk of horn or wood was inserted down the front to ensure total rigidity. The breasts were flattened into submission, and the waist was constricted to absurdly dainty dimensions. Iron corsets, triumphs of the blacksmith's art, survive from this period, although several fashion historians believe that these torturous contraptions were special orthopedic supports and not representative of what was normally worn.

Hooped petticoats were still popular. France and England, as might be expected, preserved the French wheel-shaped farthingale, although the simple bum roll was becoming increasingly acceptable, even among women of quality. Spain, Italy, the Spanish Netherlands, and Habsburg Austria kept to the rigid cone shape of the Spanish farthingale. The waistline, in either style, remained long and pointed. Long, hanging false sleeves, cut in many intricate ways, were still seen on court costumes, especially in areas under Spanish influence. Necklines varied. Spanish costume still insisted on total coverage, with a high-standing collar extending right up under the closed ruff. Elsewhere—particularly France and England—extreme décolletage was usual, the neckline often being cut as low as the nipples. In such cases, however, a light scarf or semisheer undergarment usually preserved a semblance of modesty. English woodcuts of the period show the breasts entirely exposed, but the intent appears to have been satirical rather than factual.

When Louis XIII attained his majority he ruled ineptly for a few years, then with obvious relief turned the government over to his able minister, Cardinal Richelieu, while he himself alternately pursued game, women, and fashion. Richelieu's successes were spectacular. He reestablished French prestige, confirmed the absolute power of the monarchy, and through improved administration created a truly centralized government. French fashions, equally spectacular, spread throughout Europe, reflecting and reinforcing France's new international image.

Under Louis XIII the nobility went to reckless extremes in the pursuit of status through fashion, vainly attempting to outdo the sartorial splendor of the rich bourgeoisie. The earlier years of Louis's reign were marked by costumes of extraordinary opulence and overindulgence. Rich imported fabrics flooded the court in defiance of the taxes and sumptuary laws of the previous monarchs. Then in 1625 Richelieu promulgated the first of a series of edicts that were to have a profound effect on the development of French costume. Once again imported textiles were banned, and the fashion-conscious courtiers and upper bourgeoisie were forced to rely on the products of local industry.

The last elements of Spanish fashion began to disappear and soon they were gone altogether, replaced by new modes. The nobility, having little else to do after Richelieu deprived them of their political power, took the lead in the development of new fads, but they were closely followed by the wealthy townsmen. Sumptuary laws intended to restrict extremes of fashion to the nobility were generally ignored, and during the reign of Louis XIII it was virtually impossible to distinguish between the aristocracy and the upper middle class on the basis of their clothing.

Men's clothing changed radically. The peasecod belly and the over-inflated sleeves joined the codpiece in the limbo of lost fashions. The doublet fit more closely to the body. The waistline was fairly high and less pointed; the skirts of the garment, usually cut in several sections, fell well below the hips. Shirts of fine linen or silk were exposed through slashes in the doublet sleeve. The ruff was no longer worn. Men wore instead a wide-falling collar of fine linen deeply bordered with lace. Breeches were slimmer in cut and reached well below the knees, where the hose were laced on with points. Square-toed, low-cut shoes were worn indoors, but they were almost equaled in popularity by boots with huge, floppy turned-down cuffs. Boot hose of plain

By the middle of the seventeenth century the long dominance of Spain and Spanish fashion was on the wane throughout Europe. The high collar and full ruff had given way to the wide-falling collar, and the peasecod belly to softer, more natural lines, as evidenced in the portrait of the duke of Orléans seen at right.

cloth, trimmed at the top with lace matching that of the collar, were worn over the silk hose to protect them from the oils of the leather.

Decoration was still lavish, but made up of less expensive materials. Dozens of bows, miles of braid, and regiments of buttons replaced the gem-encrusted gold bullion of the previous era. Capes were generally worn as outer wraps. In the French style, they were draped nonchalantly over the left shoulder in a manner that appeared to defy the laws of gravity. They were in fact firmly secured by a cord stitched under the collar, brought around the shoulders under the falling collar of the doublet and then tied in back. Wide-brimmed felt hats trimmed with ostrich feathers were fashionable, and the dashing costume was completed by the court sword, hung from a wide baldric across the right shoulder, and by the waved and curled lovelocks of the young chevalier. The costume was splendid, highly attractive, and—perhaps of greater significance—it was reasonably comfortable, cut on easy and generous lines to permit freedom of movement.

Women's costume reflected this new concern for elegance and comfort. Many layers of clothing were still worn: a well-dressed woman wore, next to her skin, a chemise and long Italianate drawers or breeches to which her hose could be attached by points; the drawers were also fitted with pockets, which were reached through discreet slits in the seams of the outer garments; next came several petticoats and at times a light corset. The outermost petticoat was made of fine fabric, intended to be seen when the skirts of the gown were lifted for ease in walking. The other items of underwear were made of delicate linen, although wool or flannel petticoats might be worn in winter. The two-piece gown was next, usually cut from soft, light-colored satins or brocades. The full skirts fell normally to the floor, for by this time even the bum roll was in decline. The bodice was high-waisted with a short peplum falling over the top of the skirt. The full puffed sleeves were now sewn to the bodice rather than being laced on with points. The bodice was often stiffly boned above the waistline, doing away with the need for a separate corset. The stomacher—the central front of the bodice—was often cut separately. It curved generously over the abdomen, emphasizing fecund roundness. Finally, an open robe, usually cut from fine black velvet, went over all. The sleeves of the robe were entirely open from shoulder to wrist to expose the bodice sleeves. Ribbons, often ornamented with huge rosettes, held the gown at the waist and caught the sleeves at the elbow. The necklines of both bodice and robe were deeply cut, then usually filled in with several layers of gauze or lawn. Wide, lace-trimmed collars and turned-up cuffs completed the costume. At home, the robe was often laid aside and the fine gown protected by a long apron.

The styles for both men and women were rich, elegant, and dignified, at times having an almost classical simplicity. The high waist gave the impression of long, graceful legs; and soft, natural contours contrasted strongly with the constricted rigidity of the previous generation. Wide lace and linen collars focused attention on the face without giving the effect of grotesque isolation that resulted when the head was balanced in the middle of a huge cartwheel ruff. Hairstyles were generally restrained, and superfluous ornamentation had all but disappeared.

The new mode spread to England, encouraged by Henrietta Maria, queen to Charles I and sister of Louis XIII. By and large, English styles were more conservative. Sleeves were shorter and softer in outline, and the velvet outer robe was hardly ever worn. In Holland the styles were avidly followed by young people, while the older generation remained faithful to the severe fashions of the turn of the century. The mercurial rise of Dutch trade and the expansion of the overseas commercial empire brought new wealth into the small country, still newly rejoicing in its hard-won independence from Spain. By around 1635 almost all the Spanish elements of costume had been abandoned in favor of the new, easy French styles, which remained in vogue until the early years of the eighteenth century.

As a rule, Dutch fashions were never as colorful or as ostentatious as their French prototypes; plain, solid colors often enriched with fur were preferred over figured brocades and damasks. Now and again, religious strictures against "vanity in dress" were invoked, causing considerable harm to the local textile industries. Only one aspect of Dutch costume indicated the earlier dominance of Spain: the overwhelming preference for black. Although black had been the favorite color of the hated Spanish papists, the Dutch Calvinists associated its understated sobriety with their own austere religion.

Spain adhered stubbornly to late sixteenth-century styles until around 1630, when a noticeable thaw set in. Elements of French style were introduced but were more pronounced in male than in female attire. With the exception of gala court dress, fabrics tended to be plain and heavily encrusted with braid or passementeries. Philip III, consistently orthodox in his religion, had wrecked the Spanish textile industry by his expulsion of the Moorish craftsmen in 1609, after which patterned textiles became increasingly rare. Gold and silver from the New World still flowed into Spain but this became stagnant, rather than circulating, wealth. Spanish society was sharply divided, ruled by the court and by grandees and officials connected, however distantly, with the Crown. The burden of the Spanish economy was borne by everyone else—merchants, artisans, and peasants—those not protected by royal favor. Most of the numerous and rigidly enforced sumptuary laws of Spain were directed against the commoners. The freedom of Paris, where nobility and bourgeoisie vied in the field of fashion, would have been unthinkable in Madrid.

At the time of the death of Louis XIII, all Europe, with the exception of Spain, imitated French culture and copied French fashions. During the long reign of Louis XIV (1643–1715), France emerged as the strongest and wealthiest state in Europe. The political ascendency achieved during this period lasted throughout the greater part of the eighteenth century. The cultural dominance established during this reign lasted still longer. In fact, until the third decade of the nineteenth century France virtually dictated European styles in architecture, painting, literature, drama, language, manners, and dress. The taste of all Europe was decreed by the Sun King and his brilliant court.

Louis looked upon kingship not merely as an inherited right but as an exacting profession, the *métier du roi*. Every waking moment was absorbed in acting out to the fullest the role of king. A splendid royal figure emerges from the histories of the seventeenth century; the man himself remains, to a large extent, an enigma. Historians agree as to the superficial image of the Sun King; they disagree sharply about his true character and the value of his accomplishments. To some, Louis figures as the most outstanding ruler of the modern era; to others, he appears mediocre and ineffectual, a concentration of vanities in human form. The truth, as usual, seems to lie somewhere in between.

Louis was not quite five years old when his father died and his Spanish Habsburg mother, Anne of Austria, was appointed regent of France. Anne was entirely dependent upon Cardinal Mazarin, the pupil and spiritual heir of the great Richelieu. Although Louis attained his major-

Less frequently displayed but no less splendidly made was the underwear worn beneath a seventeenth-century nobleman's court dress. This set, made from fine linen embroidered with colored silk and outlined in gold and silver thread, was originally part of a young courtier's trousseau.

ity at the age of fourteen, he continued to depend on the advice and guidance of Mazarin. But when the cardinal died in 1661, Louis took the government directly into his own hands. The court, remembering Louis's pleasure-loving father and the weak and dissolute sons of Henry II, fully expected that after a week or two of playing king, the young man would choose a new prime minister and return to a more relaxed way of life. The court had sadly underestimated its king. Louis's one ambition was to assume full power and he permitted nothing to interfere with this intent, not even the incredible load of hard and unremitting work that he carried for the rest of his life.

Until around 1650, costume remained in a state of transition; the handsome and noble styles of the previous reign were followed with some modification of ornament in accordance with new sumptuary laws, which banned all trimming except silk ribbons. Then, suddenly, petticoat breeches or rhinegraves burst upon the scene; wide, open-legged trousers so full that they looked like skirts, reaching down to the knee or even to mid-calf. These curious garments apparently originated in Germany and may have been introduced to the French court by the eccentric Count Palatine Edward, who was married to a lady in waiting to Anne of Austria.

The petticoat breeches were worn with a matching doublet, cut short so that the shirt would show between doublet and breeches. The doublet was commonly left unbuttoned or only partially buttoned to allow even more of the shirt to emerge. The doublet sleeves are quite curious; composed of narrow strips of brocade lined with white taffeta, they were attached only at the armholes and the short cuff, exposing still more of the shirt. Yard upon yard of ribbon decorate the doublet cuffs, the waistline, and the sides of the breeches. Often more than 250 yards of ribbon were required to decorate these monstrosities.

The shirts worn with these outfits were of fine linen or silk, with huge, full sleeves, heavily bedecked with ruches, ruffles, lace, and more ribbon. Odd-looking ruffles of linen and lace, called cannons, were worn just below the ribbons of the breeches, falling over embroidered silk stockings. Along with all this one wore a short, full cape and a hat loaded with ostrich plumes. Shoes with high red heels and stiff butterfly bows were commonly worn, although low, bucket-topped boots were acceptable for street wear. Louis is often erroneously credited with having invented high heels; in fact they had been around since the middle of the sixteenth century. His approval of the fashion caused a resurgence of its popularity. (He himself was around five feet four inches tall and needed all the extra altitude he could get.) Wigs, often of prodigious dimensions, were worn over shaved scalps, although Louis himself refused to sacrifice his own abundant hair until the 1670's.

This absurd costume, based on trousers originated by the somewhat addled Count Palatine, was enthusiastically supported by Louis and his sycophants, and it remained in fashion until about 1680. But Louis had good reasons for encouraging a mode that caused gentlemen to look like refugees from an explosion in a ribbon factory: the fashion required yards of fabric, miles of ribbon, and acres of lace, all now produced in France. From the 1640's on, Mazarin had published and

In Hyacinthe Rigaud's famous portrait, Louis XIV of France is accoutered in a manner befitting the preeminent monarch of seventeenth-century Europe. His cascading robes, lined in ermine and emblazoned with golden fleurs-de-lis, bespeak regality in their every detail. This royal court costume was patterned on men's formal attire of the late sixteenth century and only a few details, such as the cravat, reflect contemporary early eighteenth-century fashions.

enforced a series of sumptuary laws banning imported embroideries, cloth of gold and silver, and Flemish and Venetian laces.

One of Louis's first independent acts after Mazarin's death was to reconfirm this ban on imports. He himself scrupulously observed these restrictions, setting his court a much needed example. At the same time, acting on the advice of his minister Colbert, he recruited skilled Venetian craftsmen and settled them throughout France. Alençon, Arras, Rheims, Château-Thierry, Loudon, and other cities became the centers of a new and flourishing industry. Gold and silver braids and trimmings were also produced but were restricted to the nobility, who were encouraged to use them with abandon.

This new fashion was well under way by 1660 when Louis married Marie Thérèse of Spain, daughter of Philip IV. Spain, predictably, had not accepted these styles; tapestries and paintings recording the marriage show the grandees in conservative and rather old-fashioned attire of a cut popular in the 1630's. Spanish female court costume, on the other hand, more than compensated for this lack of flair. The old cone-shaped farthingale had continued in fashion until around 1640 when a new skirt support, the garde-infante, was introduced. Mme de Motteville described one: "Their garde-infante was a circular machine and a monstrous one, for it was like several barrel hoops sewn into the skirt, except that hoops are round and their garde-infante was flattened at the front and behind, and spread out at the sides."

Spanish women were more severely corseted than ever, if possible; little girls were squashed inside tight stays at an early age to prevent the natural development of their breasts. The grotesque hoops shot straight out on either side of the waist to a width greater than the reach of the arms. Spanish ladies were taught to walk with delicate mincing steps so that they seemed to roll along on casters. As its name indicates, the garde-infante was reserved for women of the royal family and the

During Louis XIV's long reign his magnificent palace at Versailles was the political and social nexus of Western Europe. Through its numerous reception rooms—seen above in a series of contemporary engravings by Antoine Trouvain—moved the most splendidly dressed courtiers on the Continent. As these views indicate, many of them favored complicated coiffeurs and pale complexions accented by dark beauty patches. Among the better-known residents of Versailles was Mme Louise de la Vallière (opposite), the king's mistress, who bore Louis three children.

court; lesser mortals fell back on the bum roll. As an outward sign of her new allegiance, Marie Thérèse changed to French garments when she arrived on French soil. At first she felt awkward and embarrassed, but etiquette required that she wear the costume of her new homeland, and she eventually became accustomed to it.

French female costume of the 1660's was not so extreme as the fantastic outfits worn by men. The basic dress was the bodice and skirt, still usually designed as two garments. The waistline was dropped to a relatively normal position in back and drawn down to a low, sharp point in front. The bodice was heavily boned and tight fitting. Sleeves were quite short and full, but the arms were covered to well below the elbow by the full flounced sleeves of the chemise. The skirt was usually split down the front to expose the underskirt, and the looped-up folds of the train were often bunched and fastened in back. The length of the train, like almost everything else at Louis's court, was determined by the rank of the wearer. Gowns usually had a wide bateau neckline, filled in with lace or a gauze fichu. Women no longer wore underdrawers and their absence inspired many a merry jest when ladies took a tumble during the hunt. Some opportunists among the fair sex were rumored to have deliberately engineered such happy accidents.

Women's fashions were set, not by Louis's queen, but by his mistresses. Mme de Montespan introduced a soft, relatively unboned negligee or *robe de chambre*, allegedly to disguise her numerous pregnancies. Louise de la Vallière contributed the necklace that still bears her name, and Mlle de Fontanges developed a new hairstyle. Cosmetics were used by both men and women, as were beauty patches. The patches might be simple dots, artfully placed to call attention to fine eyes or a succulent mouth, or they might be cut in stars, crescents, or other exotic shapes. They emphasized the porcelain whiteness of the skin and were also useful for masking syphilitic eruptions and acne.

Versailles in its heyday was a tableau vivant without parallel in all of Europe. The course of Continental fashion was charted in the grand salons of the palace (right), even as the political destiny of the West was being determined in its state apartments.

The French court at Versailles became the fashion center of all Europe. Versailles was a splendid theater where Louis and his courtiers acted out the never-ending pageant of the Sun King in all his glory. It also served as a great gilded cage to contain the nobility of France. In the old and bitter rivalry between king and aristocracy over feudal pretensions to power, Louis succeeded where many of his predecessors had failed. The great nobles were politely invited to partake of the royal hospitality of Versailles where, of course, the king could supervise their activities. The personal favor of the monarch was the only key to success in this glittering and artificial world, and to attain this favor it was necessary to be in attendance at all times.

The life of a courtier at Versailles was one of frenetic and grueling

social duty, of rising at six and, if fortunate, retiring at midnight; of constant attendance upon the king, long days spent standing and walking through seemingly endless rooms and corridors. Court life was an eternal and exhausting round of balls, parties, and banquets, of masques and pageants, of chapel-going and rides in the park. All these activities required frequent changes of costume and occasionally Louis would require the courtiers to fit themselves out in a new wardrobe for a special occasion, such as a royal birth or wedding. Rigid and complicated etiquette preserved order among the throngs of courtiers. Serious topics of discussion meant instant disfavor; conversations were limited to scandals and fashions. Louis had never forgotten his childhood when the rebellion of the Fronde had almost cost him his throne. His nobles, safely under his watchful eye and encouraged to strip their estates to cover their backs, were not likely to pose any such threat again.

In the early 1680's, the mindless frivolity of the court was dampened by a new and perhaps welcome atmosphere of sobriety and decorum. The king had tired of the overwhelming arrogance and bad temper of his chief mistress, Mme de Montespan; perhaps more to the point, she began to lose her figure after the birth of their last child. Her involvement in the scandalous poison affair had further aroused his alarm and although the king managed to shield her reputation, she was no longer welcome at court. The royal affections were transferred to the ultra-respectable Mme de Maintenon, governess to the royal bastards; and sometime after the death of the queen in 1683, she became the king's wife. Mme de Maintenon, perhaps as a legacy of her obscure middle-class origins, was strait-laced and obsessively pious. But Louis himself was beginning to feel his years, and her quiet wit and refinement must have been a welcome change from the hysterics, tantrums, and general stupidity of his previous inamoratas.

French fashions were quick to reflect this new state of affairs. Petticoat breeches and other extravagances of attire vanished almost overnight and were replaced by costumes equally sumptuous but far more restrained and understated. The justaucorps or waistcoat, which had been worn for about twenty years, was redesigned and emerged as the most distinctive article of male attire. It was a knee-length tailored coat with a fitted waistline and flared skirts that were stiffened to stand away from the figure. It had long sleeves with wide cuffs and was ornamented with braid and a great many buttons and buttonholes, both functional and nonfunctional. It had no collar, which, in any case, would have been hidden by the full wig. It was worn with a sleeveless vest, also knee length, and closefitting knee-length breeches. Lace and linen cravats were worn to conceal the front opening of the shirt.

As early perhaps as 1662, Louis himself designed a special justaucorps, blue with red lining and ornaments and worn with a red vest, both garments heavily embroidered in gold. These coats were given to especially favored courtiers, but according to the Duc de Saint-Simon, neither the king nor the Grand Dauphin wore this get-up. By the time Saint-Simon arrived at court in 1691, the king's personal preference in costume had become downright stodgy: "The King always wore plain brown, sometimes set off by a gold button or a bit of black velvet. He wore an open vest of embroidered cloth or satin, either blue or red. He shunned rings and wore jewels only on his shoe buckles, his garters and his hat, which was trimmed in Spanish needlepoint and decorated with a white plume." The courtiers were by no means limited to such a somber palette, although their garments were cut along the same conservative lines. Behavior also was conservative; libertinism, formerly winked at, was now officially disapproved of although it continued unabated behind the king's back.

Women's fashions also became more stiff and formal. Gowns were cut along the same basic patterns of the previous period, but the silhouette changed radically. The front edges of the trained overskirt were pulled farther to the back of the figure and looped up at intervals to

A representative example of the refined craftsmanship of eighteenth-century French tailors, this mauve silk gentlemen's suit is embellished with an overall design of white flowers linked by green foliage.

fall in classic festoons. The mass of material at the rear was further accentuated by a bustle, a modified bum roll with the fullness concentrated at central back. The exposed underskirt was richly ornamented, usually with horizontal bands of braid or tiers of ruffles or lace. The stiff-boned bodice fell to a decided point in front and décolletage was still extreme, despite Mme de Maintenon's insistence upon a more modest neckline. The costume was not particularly comfortable and was almost impossible to sit in except on low stools or cushions on the floor. Since, however, only a very few women at court were entitled to a chair, such considerations were unimportant. The ruffles and ruches of the fontanges headdress scaled ever greater heights; its popularity had considerably outlasted that of its fair inventor.

Louis XIV gave France its most splendid era of national glory, although he almost destroyed the country in the process. When, in 1715, he lay on his deathbed, the country was bankrupt from the drain of his devastating wars and his exhausting building programs. The people were destitute; the population itself was reduced; commerce and trade were fettered by unreasonable taxation; the Calvinist Huguenots, the most productive members of the middle class, had been driven into exile; the bourgeoisie was restless; and the aristocracy had lost the administrative usefulness it had once possessed.

The news of his death was heard with great relief by the people, who had been plunged into misery by their ruler's extravagance and ambition. His body was rushed into the grave with a minimum of ceremony and, according to Voltaire, there was dancing in the streets of Paris. Later generations have been kinder to him, for misery passes, eventually, and splendor remains.

The throne devolved upon the late king's great grandson, Louis XV, a child five years of age. The regent, Philippe of Orléans, closed the great châteaux of Versailles and Marly—a gesture that saved millions for the sagging economy—and moved to the Palais Royal in the center of Paris. The social life of the Paris salons—gay, witty, informal —formed a welcome contrast to the frigid etiquette of Versailles. The young king returned to Versailles after the regent's death, but the relationship between the court and the upper bourgeoisie remained close.

The general reaction against extreme formality was mirrored in the fashions of the new regime. With an almost audible sigh of relief, much of the stiffness drained out of women's clothing and was replaced by the graceful, fluid lines so well illustrated in the paintings of Watteau. The style apparently was derived from the *robe de chambre* of the previous reign, a relaxed and informal dress that could be worn only in the privacy of the home. The basic line, capable of many variations, was a loose dress worn over a tight bodice and a full underskirt or petticoat. The Watteau gown or sack dress featured double box pleats set in on a straight-back neckline to fall unbelted to the ground in a train. In front, the pleats converged to a point low on the waistline with the opening either sewn or caught together with bows. It could also be worn open in front to show the petticoat, which was often cut from the same material. Boned bodices and stomachers were worn, cut low to expose a great deal of delicate bosom. Sleeves were elbow length with vertical

pleats, echoing the motif of the back pleats, and terminated in soft, wide cuffs over the lacy frills of the chemise sleeve. Skirts were bell-shaped, supported by a hooped petticoat. The hoops did not extend all the way to the floor like the old farthingale; they ended a bit below the knee, allowing the skirt to fall in softer folds. Hairstyles were simple and neat, fairly close to the head; small frilled caps were worn.

One of the more obvious changes in fashion was the choice of material. The older generation had preferred heavy fabrics; sturdy silks, satins, and velvets that could be tailored and draped in formal lines, in consistently dark, rich colors. The new styles called for lighter fabrics, delicate silks and damasks; chintz and Indian cottons—printed, painted, embroidered, or plain—were worn even by the wealthy. Colors were lighter, and a decided preference for soft pastels appeared. The overall look was warmly appealing, simple, graceful, and almost childlike.

Many examples of actual textiles of this period have been preserved. Eighteenth-century silks were as expensive as they were gorgeous, and the material—for all its superficial delicacy—was unusually tough and durable. When a gown fell out of fashion it was laid away to await a future glorious resurrection when it would be taken apart and restyled. A typical sack dress and petticoat, for example, used about twenty yards of material, most of which ran in long, uncut panels from neck to hem. It could be progressively remodeled from decade to decade, or laid out flat and completely recut in a brand new mode. Lyons silks from the 1740's can often be traced through any number of reincarnations; from the original sack to a *robe à l'anglaise* or a polonaise of the 1770's, thence to a high-waisted empire gown of the early 1800's, a day dress of the 1830's, or an evening dress of the 1890's. This recycling of eighteenth-century fabric was most active in the 1840's when delicately figured floral silks were fashionable again. After that decade, most alterations were for the creation of fancy-dress ball gowns rather than for serious wear.

Men's costume remained fairly homogeneous throughout most of the eighteenth century and consisted of the basic items of coat, vest, and breeches that had come into favor late in the reign of Louis XIV. While women's garments became more ornate and complex, the general lines of men's wear were increasingly simplified, resulting in a neat, well-tailored silhouette. Coats were cut and curved away in front and gradually lost their fullness at the sides. The vest, also closely fitted, grew progressively shorter as the century wore on and was cut away in front to form a deep inverted triangle. Breeches were tighter and more elegant in cut, closely buttoned at the side of the knee. The coat and, if necessary, the breeches were padded and shaped to produce rounded, smooth forms. Stocking pads of lamb's wool were available to plump out shrunken calves, and real dandies wore corsets or stays to give them a more military bearing.

By mid-century, female fashions were dictated by Mme de Pompadour, Louis XV's *maîtresse en titre*, whose semiofficial reign lasted from 1745 until her death in 1764. Witty, elegant, and amusing, she was the real power behind the throne, for Louis—unlike his great-grandfather,

The Marquise de Montespan, often pregnant during her long liaison with Louis XIV, took to wearing a loose-fitting negligee, or robe de chambre, to hide her distended abdomen. A graceful, fluid style, it was to evolve into the sack dress featured in the Watteau painting at left. Another royal mistress, Louis XV's Marquise de Pompadour, ruled unchallenged over Versailles and French fashion for twenty years, a suzerainty that ended only with her death in 1764. In the portrait below she wears the robe à la française *that she popularized during her lifetime.*

who never allowed any of his women to influence him politically—was easily led. Pompadour, ambitious and politically naïve, was susceptible to the suggestions of every plausible opportunist or office seeker swarming around the remunerative hive of Versailles. Despite the slanders of her detractors, she was neither vicious nor stupid. Expensively educated, she was an ardent disciple of the new learning of the Enlightenment and her unassailable position at court allowed her to support and protect Voltaire, Diderot, and other *philosophes* and encyclopedists. The sophisticated naïveté that characterizes the French rococo was to a great extent a direct reflection of her own exquisitely refined taste.

● In the field of costume, Pompadour brought the *robe à la française* to such a state of perfection that it practically became the French national costume. This dress was derived from the earlier sack gown with the pleated back train and the overskirt split over a petticoat. It was worn over elliptical hoops or paniers, which concentrated the fullness at the sides only, leaving both the front and the rear of the gown quite flat. At home, the paniers were often omitted. The fullness was then controlled by pulling the front corners of the robe up through the pocket holes to form great swags of drapery on either side. Pockets were separate items, pouch-shaped bags stitched to a band tied around the waist under the petticoat; they were reached through slits in the outer clothing. The stomacher of the tight bodice was filled in with a mass of graduated bows, and more bows decorated the sleeves over the voluminous frills of the delicate lace cuffs.

Fabrics, both plain and patterned, were soft and fragile; colors were clear and bright and were given highly imaginative names: flea's head, nymph's thighs, nun's belly, poisoned monkey, lovesick frog, distressed toad, frightened mouse. Jewelry was restrained; a few matchless pearls at neck, ears, or wrist were considered quite sufficient. A frilly lace choker or a pert pussycat bow matching the gown were often worn instead of a necklace. The hair was dressed neatly and usually powdered. Flowers, both real and artificial, might be worn in the hair or on the gown for further decoration. The *robe à la française* was worn by all women, varying only in the choice of material and the volume of the hoops. The style remained popular until well into the 1770's.

An extreme version of the gown, with extraordinarily wide and stiffly boned paniers, a narrow pointed bodice, and a long train was retained even longer as formal court costume. Court dress was unusually heavy and cumbersome and forced the wearer to move in a slow, stately glide. According to Casanova, when the court ladies were required to hurry, they lifted their hoops to their chins, bent their knees and hopped along like kangaroos.

During the seventeenth century, French styles were spread throughout Europe by the means of fashion dolls. These little female figures, designed in adult proportions, were carefully coiffured and dressed in miniature replicas of the latest modes. They were usually made up by leading Parisian modistes, and even as late as the 1770's Marie Antoinette's dressmaker, Rose Bertin, toured the Continent each year in the off season in a carriage stuffed with the little poppets. The dolls not only advertised the current styles, but fabrics as well, for their

tiny dresses were cut from the finest textiles produced in France. Few of these exquisite miniatures have survived; after they had served their original purpose they were handed down to little girls as toys and subsequently loved to death.

During the reign of Louis XIV the *Mercure Galant* was the sole publication dealing with matters of fashion. Its timely advice was supplemented by *Le Tailleur Sincère*, a technical treatise devoted to pattern drafting and to an occasional series of engravings depicting prominent figures of society. True fashion journals did not appear until the 1760's, when they seemed to burst forth spontaneously in Paris and London, closely followed by German, Dutch, and Italian periodicals. The French publications—*Journal du Goût, Cabinet des Modes, Magasin des Modes nouvelles, Courrier de la Mode, La Gallerie des Modes* —were by far the most influential and were widely circulated. The plates were beautifully engraved and often hand-colored. Specialized journals, dedicated to hairdressing, corsetry, embroidery, and exotic needlework appeared at about the same time. With these periodicals, a

clever modiste in a provincial town or a foreign country could turn out costumes equal to those paraded at Versailles.

These journals also brought about rapid changes in fashion. In the seventeenth century or in the first half of the eighteenth, styles changed gradually; a particularly successful mode would retain its popularity for a decade or more. Now, styles changed from one season to the next in a constant parade of new fads; gowns *à l'anglaise, à l'insurgente, à la polonaise, à la circassienne, à la créole, à la levantine, à la sultane, à la turque, à la lévite* succeeded each other with bewildering rapidity. In general, these styles indicate a trend toward more comfortable costume for women, each new mode being softer and easier in fit than its predecessor. But through their excessive mutability, the fashions also point up the restlessness of French society, the boredom and ennui that characterize the final decades of *l'ancien régime*.

A wave of Anglomania brought English fashions to France. The *robe à l'anglaise*, introduced around 1775, was boned closely to the waist and worn without paniers or hoops. The false bottom—or *cul de Paris*, a revised bum roll—held out the fullness at the back. The skirt was gathered at the hips and had a short train. It was extremely popular and was universally worn as an at-home dress while the *robe à la française* was reserved for balls, the opera, and other formal occasions. Another foreign costume, the polonaise, was brought in at about the same time. A short gown, reaching well above the ankle, it was worn over modest hoops or paniers. The overskirt, heavily flounced, was hiked up by drawstrings to form three rounded, puffed swags, one at each side and one in the rear. It is fairly typical of what Marie Antoinette wore when playing milkmaid at the Hameau.

With the accession of Louis XVI and his beautiful Austrian bride, Marie Antoinette (above), fashion once more became a matter of serious concern in the French capital. The sheer beauty of much of late eighteenth-century French costume is evident in the contemporary fashion plate opposite; the uncounted hours of hand stitching necessary to create those garments is the subject of the painting at lower right.

Once the *robe à l'anglaise* achieved the initial breakthrough, even more comfortable costumes were adopted for private wear, although they would not have done for formal appearances. The *robe à la créole* supposedly copied the gowns worn by French ladies in the Americas. It was an extremely simple dress, scarcely more than a chemise, caught in at the waist with a wide sash. It was also called a gaulle or a baby dress and was generally made up in delicate white muslin or gauze and worn without hoops over light petticoats. It could be worn with or without stays, although some sort of support was usually retained. Marie Antoinette had her portrait done wearing a gaulle; to her surprise, the painting occasioned vicious lampoons in the underground press and the canvas had to be removed from exhibition. To the revolutionaries, the lighthearted informality of the dress was insulting, even more objectionable than expensive court costume.

Costumes of the 1770's, as if in subconscious anticipation of a final fling before the deluge, were quite incredible. They were largely inspired by the frivolous and theatrical taste of the young queen, aided and abetted by the first of the great name designers, Rose Bertin, who had never heard of the axiom that less is more. The basic cut of costume did not change appreciably, but all aspects of design and decoration were carried to extremes of questionable taste. Hoops not only spread, they arched abruptly upward at the waistline. The breasts were pushed up and the neckline dropped right down to the level of the nipples, which were barely veiled by lace frills. A type of decoration called plastics was invented; this consisted of a series of swags and garlands, heavily padded with lamb's wool to stand away from the fabric of the gown. Ruffles, lace, tassels, fringe, plumes, ropes of beads, and festoons of artificial flowers, miles of fringe and ribbon—all were used with abandon.

The costume was completed by fantastic hairstyles, grotesque beyond belief. The hair, vastly augmented with switches, braids, and rats, was brushed up over huge towers of wire and crinoline, slathered with pomade and dredged with flour until it had the consistency of papier-mâché, then loaded with flowers, plumes, ribbons, veils, and all sorts of odds and ends. Miniature tableaux, landscapes, and seascapes were set forth among the curls and poufs; it was said that the best ships in the French navy were on the queen's head. The very wealthy and idle changed hairstyles frequently, but a well-constructed headdress could be cosseted along for three or four weeks. Lice and other vermin had a field day. If the itching became too severe, a lady would have her head opened; that is, slits would be made in the concretion and ivory wands inserted for a comforting scratch. An incredible collapsible bonnet, the calash, was engineered to protect these edifices, and many other varieties of hats and bonnets were also popular. Sedan chairs were apparently designed with hinged tops to accommodate these monstrosities, and in England, the main entrance to St. Paul's Cathedral was raised four feet to allow the court ladies to enter without damaging their towering coiffures.

Hairstyles, even more than costume, characterize the hectic fashions of pre-Revolutionary France. Although the nation's economy was in an

It must have seemed to contemporary critics that the worst excesses of the pre-Revolutionary age were summarized in the court costumes of the day. At a time when few Frenchmen could afford bread, let alone the cake their frivolous queen urged them to eat in its stead, royal dress reached new heights of extravagant excess. As these fashion plates from the late 1700's indicate, upswept coiffeurs of unprecedented complexity all but eclipsed fashion itself in the last years of the French monarchy.

unspeakable condition and many of the great nobles were up to their aristocratic ears in debt, money seemed plentiful; no caprice was too extravagant, no luxury too dear, no frivolity too absurd. While the poor were wondering where their next loaf of bread was coming from and the upper bourgeoisie were writhing under a disproportionate tax burden, the aristocracy continued its unbridled pursuit of fashion, scandalizing the socially conscious and enriching a small army of modistes, tailors, jewelers, and hairstylists who, with considerable agility, later managed to escape the forthcoming holocaust that was to swallow up so many of their titled patrons. Marie Antoinette's favorite hairdresser was a certain Léonard, who was so much in her confidence that he was entrusted with important details of the abortive flight of the royal family in 1791. He was not a very adept conspirator; the royal coach was apprehended at Varennes, but he himself escaped to further his career at the Russian court at St. Petersburg. Marie's modiste, Rose Bertin, also fled before the Reign of Terror and continued to practice her trade in London, padding out her considerable profits with scandalous and generally unreliable memoirs of *l'ancien régime*.

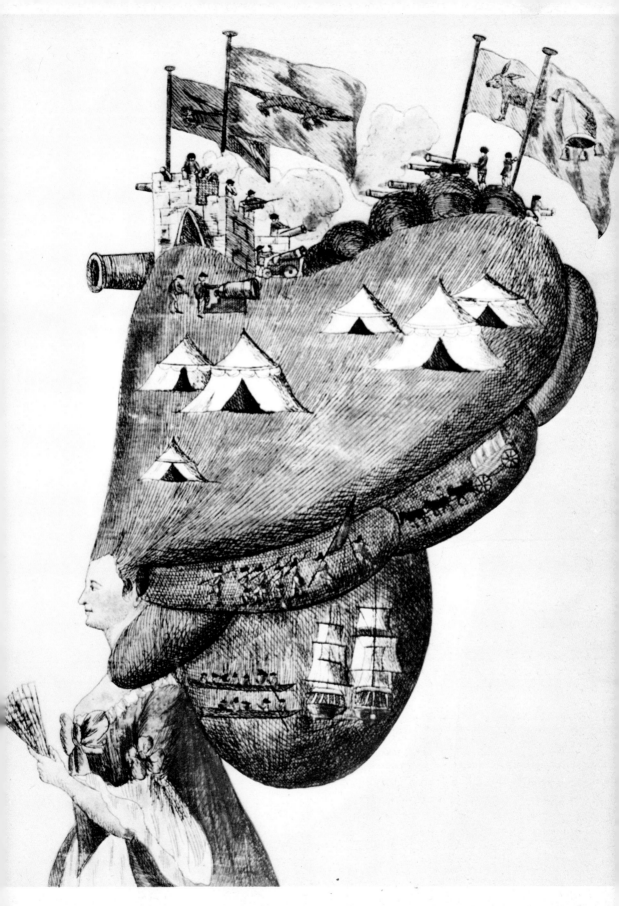

7

Haute Couture Comes of Age

Costume underwent a revolution of its own in the decades following the fall of Louis XVI, as a vogue for simple, neoclassical styles supplanted the ostentation of an earlier age. High-waisted dresses of Indian muslin, diaphanous and clinging (opposite), characterized this new mode à la greque—and incidentally revealed the female figure more completely than it had been since ancient Egyptian times.

THE LONG REIGN OF LOUIS XV witnessed a steady and irrevocable decline of the prestige and power of the French monarchy both at home and abroad. The military, political, and commercial leadership of Europe was gradually assumed by England and, to a lesser degree, by Prussia. Only in cuisine, costume, and the fine arts did France still reign supreme. When Louis XVI ascended the throne in 1744, the French hoped that a young, progressive monarch would bring better days. Louis XVI was kindly, honest, sincere, and deeply concerned for the welfare of his subjects. Unfortunately, he was quite ineffectual.

Indignation against the regime arose from the inequality of political representation, the unjust distribution of taxes, and the resentment felt by the upper bourgeoisie, stifled and frustrated by the aristocracy. Contrary to popular belief, the French Revolution was not instigated by the poor, oppressed masses, but by an upper middle class that was furious at entrenched privilege based on no better claim than pedigree, and that was no longer willing to tolerate an inefficient government that hampered its ambitions.

In May 1789, the Estates-General met for the first time in 175 years. In June, the Third Estate declared itself a National Assembly and prepared to enact legislation with or without the participation of the first two estates, the clergy and the nobility. The country began to drift into anarchy. The National Assembly met in defiance of a royal edict, the government at Versailles was in a state of frozen torpor, financial depression increased, unemployment rose, and sporadic rioting intensified. In the midst of this chaos, on July 14, the Paris mob took arms and stormed the Bastille, a prison that symbolized centuries of royal tyranny. During the following weeks, ardent revolutionaries demolished the structure completely. But the rubble did not go to waste: among the ladies of the revolutionary bourgeoisie, a necklace, brooch, or bracelet of Bastille stones, elegantly mounted in gold, became a fashionable accessory of costume.

In 1792 the radicals, inflamed by Marat and recruited from the Paris slums by Danton, overthrew the National Assembly and proclaimed a republic. In January of 1793, the king was tried, found guilty of treason, and executed. The queen, various members of the royal family, priests, and moderates followed their monarch to the scaffold. During this Reign of Terror, the list of traitors, each day diminished by the guillotine, was each night augmented by the addition of new names. Extremists felt that the Revolution would not be safe until "the last king was strangled with the guts of the last priest," a charming maxim paraphrased from Rousseau.

The revolutionaries created their own styles. Women wore the simple gown *à l'anglaise*, the gaulle, or the *négligé à la patriote*—a white dress worn under a blue redingote with a red collar. Stays were out but the *cul de Paris* was still in, boldly bearing out the gown's fullness at the rear. The sans-culottes—male revolutionaries of the lower classes—took their name from the wide, floppy trousers that had long been the standard costume of the workingman. With the trousers they wore the carmagnole, a short jacket with wide collar and lapels. A red beret or a Phrygian cap of liberty topped off the outfit; tricolor cockades sprouted everywhere. Boots were worn, or even the wooden sabots of the peasantry. Most of the leaders of the Revolution dressed as usual in the knee breeches, vest, and coat of the upper bourgeoisie.

Silks and velvets were seldom seen; it really was not safe to wear luxury fabrics. Women dressed generally in muslin and men in honest broadcloth. The demagogue Robespierre favored a white waistcoat— no doubt as a symbol of his incorruptibility—with buttons engraved with tiny guillotines; unaccountably, alone among the revolutionaries, he dressed and powdered his hair in the royalist style. It is not recorded whether or not he wore the famous waistcoast when he himself was sent to the "national razor."

As might have been expected, the Revolution ruined the French fashion and textile industries. Fashionable tailors, hairstylists, and modistes, having seen which way the flag was flying, managed to take their money and run, finding shelter and a renewed career in London, Berlin, or St. Petersburg, where they frequently discovered their former aristocratic clients working as milliners, maids, or seamstresses. Ordinary craftsmen in the fashion trades were reduced to the meager leavings of public charity. The Lyon silk weavers were totally ruined; thousands of looms were idle and were to remain so until around 1812. Further, the Assembly in a fine burst of egalitarian fervor had abolished the time-tested guild system with its steps of apprentice, journeyman, and master. The results were predictable: fabrics produced during the Republic and the Directoire periods were markedly inferior.

During the Republic (1792–95) revolutionary ideals continued to be expressed through costume. Attempts were made to create a suitable style, and the artist Jacques Louis David—politically pure since, as a member of the National Convention, he had voted for the death of the king who had subsidized him for the previous ten years—designed some rather silly outfits with vaguely classical overtones. Some of his fancy-dress confections were actually worn by members of the government during the Directoire, but vanished after Napoleon's coup d'état.

The parvenue society of the Directoire (1795–99) supported several distinct styles of costume. The Merveilleuses and Incroyables did not represent the mainstream of fashion, only the lunatic fringe. The Incroyables, striving for a careless, untidy effect, wore coats and vests that were either much too large for them or, alternatively, entirely too

116

By the beginning of the nine-teenth century the women of Paris—still the fashion arbiters for all of Europe—had taken to wearing a bewildering variety of headwear. Mob caps and turbans were popular, but nothing could compete with the poke, or pok-ing-hat, whose wide brim all but hid the wearer's face. The con-temporary illustration at right shows milliners in mob caps cre-ating hats in a Parisian atelier.

Overleaf: In 1804, the same year that he was appointed court painter to Napoleon, Jacques Louis David recorded on canvas the dazzling spectacle of the French emperor's coronation.

tight. Their costume was essentially that of the average man of the period but with all details of color, cut, and ornament carried to vulgar extremes. Their hair was cut in ragged points called dog's-ears and crowned with oversized bicornes or beaver hats. The Incroyables were little better than young thugs, playing at revolution after all the real excitement had died down; an indispensable accessory of their costume was a walking stick, heavily weighted with lead. Their female compan-ions, the Merveilleuses, wore exaggerated versions of the popular neo-classic style. Even more than the men, they achieved a sloppy, careless appearance; indeed, their clothes looked as though they had been thrown on with a pitchfork.

The most significant influence on women's costume of this period was the rediscovery of classical antiquity. Knowledge of the material appearance of the classical past had expanded during the Enlighten-ment, largely because of extensive archaeological excavations at Pom-peii and Herculaneum. The revolutionary bourgeoisie took the ancient Roman world to their hearts; possibly they saw in the ruins of those essentially middle-class towns the reflection of their own comfortable existence. Republican Rome was idealized; its political system became the official model for the new French Republic, and its architectural and sculptural styles were adopted as the only fitting forms of artistic expression. The Republic evolved into the Consulate, the Consulate into the Directoire, and the Directoire into the Empire; but the glory of ancient Rome continued to inspire the rhetoric, the pageantry, the aes-thetics, and the costume of the Napoleonic era.

The neoclassic modes of the Directoire and Empire were based on the English chemise, which had been introduced in Paris around 1790. This was a long-sleeved, tubular dress, usually made up in a soft, cling-ing muslin, its shape defined by drawstrings at the neck and at the high waist. As time wore on, the sleeves became shorter, the neckline lower, and the waistline higher; the fullness of the skirt was gradually carried to the back and lengthened into a train. Decoration was held to a minimum or omitted altogether. When ornament was used it consisted of delicate bands of classical motifs: stylized ivy, honeysuckle, or the Greek meander. Daring and especially self-confident women wore the gown with nothing under it but their well-tended and lightly oiled skins, but ordinarily a chemise and stockings were worn.

By around 1803, the gathered drawstring top was replaced by a tiny, closely fitted bodice cut with a deep, square neckline; light boning appeared either in the bodice itself or in a short corset worn under the gown. Long, rectangular shawls in silk, crepe, or cashmere were draped over the gown, accentuating its antique quality. A short, fitted high-necked jacket, the spencer, was introduced and remained in vogue until about 1830. Some aspects of the Incroyable-Merveilleuse silliness persisted until well into the Empire: a tight, narrow belt—the *ceinture à la victime*—remained in vogue, and a red ribbon around the neck was often worn to indicate a relative lost to the guillotine. The short revolutionary hairstyles, cut à la Titus or à la Caracalla, were still around although by 1805 they began to yield in favor of a Grecian knot with a profusion of tiny ringlets framing the face.

Despite David's half-hearted attempts to put men into tunics, togas, and similar inanities, male costume remained based on the combination of coat, waistcoat, and breeches that had been introduced over a hundred years earlier. These garments were constantly recut and restyled, moving steadily down the road from foppishness to conservatism. Leadership in men's fashions had passed from France to England, where styles were dictated by George Brummell and the other dandies who swaggered at the court of the prince regent.

The famous Beau denounced wigs and elaborate brocades and popularized a style based on the conservative concepts of perfect fit, faultless construction, and exquisite attention to detail. He bathed frequently—itself an act of the utmost novelty—and changed his linen as often as three times a day. His cravats were starched to perfection and tied with the greatest precision. The mirrored shine of his boots was said to have been achieved by lavish applications of a polish of his own invention, well mixed with champagne.

Beau Brummell introduced the English double-breasted riding coat, cut very high in front and tailored closely to the body, to polite society. Long trousers, formerly the garb of the déclassé workingman, also appeared, they now fitted like a second skin and were buttoned at the ankle, often anchored into unwrinkled perfection by a strap passing under the instep of the boot. Knee breeches were retained for court dress, and many older men—especially scholars and those in the professions—still held to the styles of their youth. Light colors were used for the trousers—white, cream, beige, or tan—while dark blue, bottle green, or basic black was preferred for the coat. Returning émigrés introduced this elegant and restrained style to France where it was enthusiastically received. It remained in fashion even during the Anglophobic period of the Napoleonic Wars.

In 1804 Napoleon assumed the crown of empire in a ceremony of unparalleled magnificence. The Bonaparte women participated wearing sumptuous gowns designed by the painter Isabey and executed by the

famous tailor Leroy. The gowns followed the general neoclassic style of high waists and deep, square necklines, but several new elements were added. The sleeves were tight-fitting to the wrist, where they covered the back of the hand, and had a full balloon puff at the shoulder. A wired, standing Medici ruff of delicate lace rose along the sides and back of the neckline and a long court train fell from the high waistline. The fabrics were thick satins and heavy velvets, richly encrusted with gold embroidery and fringes. These were, to be sure, court dresses, but silks and velvets now appeared frequently in both formal and day costumes, the direct result of Napoleon's attempts to revive the moribund textile industry.

The pomp and splendor of the emperor's court rivaled that of the Sun King. Magnificent costumes—which used up a great deal of fabric—were required, and women were not permitted to appear at court twice in the same gown. Leroy was ordered to redesign French fashions placing special emphasis on luxury fabrics: silks and velvets from Lyon; fine linen from St. Quentin; and tulle, batiste, and lace from Valenciennes. Napoleon was not particularly interested in fashion as such—he himself dressed modestly—but he was certainly aware of fashion's role in the economy. He overlooked no detail. It is said that he had the fireplaces in the Tuileries sealed off to force the court ladies out of their flimsy muslins and into warm and costly velvets.

Napoleon's empire, vastly overextended, collapsed in 1814 and in the following year, after Waterloo, the emperor was put away for

good on the island of St. Helena while the vacillating Congress of Vienna carved up the spoils. The world of fashion was no less vacillating; the period from 1815 to 1825 was one of transition, as modistes and tailors floundered uncertainly among the last elements of neoclassicism. The changes in women's garments were subtle, but they indicated a new trend that was to culminate in the suffocatingly feminine styles of the Romantic era. Skirts were somewhat fuller with gored panels, and the hemline had risen several inches above the ankle. Decoration was more lavish, especially at the hem, where deep bands of frills, lace, ruching, puffs, and swags were laid on with a heavy hand. The waistline was somewhat lower, as if preparing to migrate back to its normal position. The neckline gradually filled in and the sleeve line began dropping off the shoulders. Corsets were back and women began to lace tightly as if to mortify the flesh that had been gloriously unrestrained for the past twenty years.

Men, too, wore corsets—heavy contraptions of canvas and whalebone that constricted the waist and forced the chest into aggressively masculine proportions. In keeping with the changes in women's styles, men's coats were cut lower in the waist; the trousers, no longer quite so tight, terminated well above the ankle to expose dashingly striped socks. The shoes for both sexes were similar, narrow heelless slippers with low-cut vamps—they look as though they must have been held on with suction cups; the leather scarcely covers the toes and just barely grips the heel.

The aftermath of the Napoleonic era found Europe in a state of profound depression, both economically and spiritually. At the Congress of Vienna, national feelings had been totally disregarded by statesmen who partitioned, dismembered, and subdivided the Continent with little or no concern for the people involved. Napoleonic rule had been neither kind nor merciful; indeed, the reverse was most often the case; yet in many areas it had in fact destroyed feudalism and the abuses generated by that system of privileged government. As the émigré nobles and monarchs returned to Spain, Italy, and Portugal, to central and eastern Europe, they were rarely greeted with demonstrations of joyful fidelity.

The middle classes in particular felt keenly the loss of opportunity and freedom which had been theirs under imperial rule. Major European cities had become heavily industrialized and dangerously overpopulated. A new social class was emerging, the urban proletariat of the factory towns. With few exceptions, the workers lived in unimaginably squalid slums wasting their lives and those of their children in the "dark, satanic mills." Armed rebellions, fired by the spirit of nationalism and with armies recruited from the teeming urban slums, first broke out in 1820 and were periodically to convulse Europe throughout the century.

The aesthetic movement known as Romanticism reflected the profound spiritual dislocation of the Industrial Revolution. Essentially, the movement was a conscious reaction against the chilly neoclassicism of the turn of the century and the intellectual purity of the Enlightenment. It exalted emotion rather than reason and tended to appeal to the less sophisticated, less intellectual taste of the vast middle class that the industrial and political revolutions had promoted to a position of economic and governmental leadership.

Above all, Romanticism was a movement of escape. The contemporary world seemed stale, dreary, stultifying, and unspeakably drab and banal. The Romantics vastly preferred "any time but now, any place but here." The far corners of space and time were ransacked to provide images of passion, excitement, glamour and adventure. Poetry, novels, paintings, and music transported the mind to India, Persia, or Egypt, to the Renaissance or the Middle Ages. Gothic novels featuring ruined castles, moaning ghosts, ambulatory skeletons, clanking chains, and swooning ladies were the rage.

Certain accessories derived from the past, such as Mary Stuart belts, Henry IV hats, or the Betsie (Elizabethan) ruff, appeared directly in the costume of the Romantic era. Even so, Romanticism in costume was more usually characterized by a general attitude rather than by specific details. Men dressed and acted the part of the passionate Byronic lover, who nobly smothered tempests within his fiery breast. According to Chateaubriand, the fashionable male had to appear "ill and sad, with something neglected about his person, neither clean-shaven nor fully bearded, but as if his beard had sprung forth during a fit of despair; locks of windblown hair, a piercing gaze; sublime, wandering fated eyes; lips curled in disdain for the human species; and a bored, Byronic heart, drowned in disgust and the mystery of being."

Male costume was especially dashing throughout the 1830's, as men swooped about in capes in a final, imaginative fling before the stodgy sobriety of the Victorian era. Heavy corseting pinched men's waists and caused their hearts to beat with more than merely romantic agony. The tailcoat and often the waistcoat as well were padded through the chest and at the shoulders. The waistcoat was cut very low in front to reveal a large expanse of shirt and cravat. Trousers were skintight from the knees up; below the knees they were somewhat looser and anchored in place by straps buckled under the instep. The trousers were now generally cut with a central-buttoned front fly, rather than with the side-buttoned rectangular panel, which still survived over a hundred years later in sailors' uniforms. The central fly was obviously more con-

The lingering influence of the Napoleonic Empire is evident in this panoramic view of a social evening at an English country house. The gentlemen in attendance wear dark velvet jackets and milk-white cravats; the ladies wear high-waisted, close-fitting dresses. The costumes are transitional, fluttering on the verge of the Romantic era.

venient; some religious leaders felt that it was entirely too convenient. When the style finally reached the American Far West, Brigham Young denounced the garments as "fornication pants" and forbade their wear among the faithful.

The Mormon leader's indignation can be measured by his use of the word "pants" in mixed company. Gentlemen in the nineteenth century did not wear pants. The wore indescribables, unspeakables, unutterables, or unthinkables; they donned nether integuments, femoral habiliments, or limb shrouders, but they most definitely did not wear pants. Neither, as a matter of fact, did they wear shirts. The mere use of the word was felt to indicate moral degeneracy. Well-bred ladies fainted at far less; the only acceptable euphemism for the garment was "linen."

The female companion of the Byronic lover was the refined and genteel lady, a strange blend of ministering angel, sprightly fairy, and blushing child; the essence of helpless, fluttering femininity; inane,

incompetent, uneducated, and cloyingly sweet. They were so unlike their mothers, the forceful, outspoken liberated women of the Revolution and the Empire, that they seemed to belong to another species altogether. As a rule, any given cultural period embodies a reaction against the manners and mores of the previous era, but seldom has the reaction been as extreme as in the 1830's when it almost assumed the proportions of a vast masculine conspiracy.

Men placed women on lofty pedestals where they perched uncomfortably throughout the rest of the nineteenth century. Women were credited with qualities of truly angelic goodness and spirituality and, in the process, were stripped of ordinary human dignity. Literature of the mid-Victorian period abounds with these delicate creatures; David Copperfield's beloved and idiotic Dora, or the absurdly self-sacrificing Little Dorrit. Strong, independent women were relegated to comic relief like Betsy Trotwood, came to a bad end like Mrs. Dombey or the unrepentant Becky Sharp or, like Jane Eyre, wound up with sloppy but well-seasoned seconds. For all their blatant femininity, the ideal females of the mid-nineteenth century were curiously unsexed; one is led to suspect a belief in parthenogenesis.

The distinguishing features of female costume of the Romantic era —full sleeves and skirts, dropped shoulders, and narrow waists—appeared around 1825 and endured, with modifications, until the 1850's. Once again women were swaddled in layer upon layer of clothing as though the freedom of the Empire had never existed. Little girls wore frilly drawers or pantalettes that peeped from under their short skirts; by the 1830's similar articles were generally worn by grown women of the middle classes although both the aristocracy and the working class tended to avoid them.

The usual basic undergarment was the chemise, a straight, unshaped linen shift that could double as a nightgown. The petticoat usually came next; if it was made with a bodice the shift might be omitted. Extra petticoats were added, either for warmth or for volume to support the skirt. They were heavily starched and corded at the bottom to give greater body. Crinoline petticoats, woven of linen and horsehair, carried the skirt to even greater dimensions. Bag pockets, reached through slits in the side seams, might be worn, and a large bustle of crimoline ruffles or padded linen was tied on at the rear. Bustles often slipped out of place, much to the amusement of bystanders. Sleeve puffs were worn on the upper arm; these were pillowlike contrivances, stuffed with down, that supported the enormous sleeves of the dress.

Corsets had achieved great technical advances; they were now cut in many intricately shaped pieces, heavily boned along each seam, and frequently padded in the bosom. They usually had steel plates in front that hooked together and metal eyelets along the back opening for lacing. If the eyelets could be made to meet, it was a sure indication that the device was too large. These fashionable prisons guaranteed that the hapless females laced therein would behave like proper ladies. Active movement was virtually impossible; injudicious efforts were often rewarded with resounding explosions as the laces gave way. Ladies drank vinegar and picked at their food to keep fashionably thin

"Unlike ordinary folk, who change their wardrobe with the seasons of the year, these elegant people appear in new creations hour by hour," wrote an observer of the fashion scene in early nineteenth-century London. The beribboned dresses of the period, with their full sleeves and fuller skirts (right), were highly theatrical in their overall effect, reflecting an enthusiasm for personal display that led such a prominent figure of the age as Lord Byron (left) to outfit himself in exotic native garb.

and pale and, at any rate, the constant tight lacing tended to produce nausea at the mere sight or smell of food. Painfully constricted, women suffered constantly from palpitations, the vapors, and swooning.

The gowns worn over these multitudinous undergarments were usually cut from delicate and buoyant materials; organdy, tarlatan, cambric, muslin, and such for summer; challis, cashmere, peau de soie, and satin for winter. Colors were muted and ladylike; delicate figured prints and stripes were popular. The necklines were high for the day; for evening wear they were fairly low, cut in a straight line across the shoulders. The shoulder line was quite low and was exaggerated by wide collars, pelerines, falling ruffles, and lace berthas. Sleeves were huge, and the leg-of-mutton shape was frequently seen. The bodice was often trimmed with diagonal folds of fabric or other ornamentation to emphasize both the sloped shoulder line and the tiny belted waist. Tiers of flounces or braid on the skirt and ridiculously wide hats augmented the generally horizontal effect.

During the 1840's, the more extreme aspects of women's fashions began to disappear. The incredible hats were the first to go, replaced

It has been said that no century was as preoccupied with style—or as devoid of real style—as the nineteenth. Certainly this was true at midcentury, when women's fashions became hopelessly fussy and imitative. Ruffles and bows abounded (left), lacing and corsetry were reintroduced (right), and extravagance was everywhere (below).

by modest bonnets tied firmly under the chin. The ballooning sleeves deflated, and the shoulder line began crawling upward toward its natural position. Skirts were fuller than ever and now swept the ground; the applied ornament was largely discarded. Heavier fabrics became popular again, and there was a distinct trend toward darker, richer, and more intense colors. The overall effect became increasingly sober, self-effacing, modest, and oppressively respectable. The spirit of Romanticism was dying and Realism was emerging in its stead.

The later nineteenth century tended to equate "truth" neither with classical rationalism nor with romantic idealism but rather with the unpleasant, pragmatic realities of the contemporary world. It was no longer possible to hide from the social disorders that had sporadically swept Europe since the 1820's. France, in particular, underwent several major changes of government: the overthrow of Charles X in 1830, the limited "bourgeois" monarchy of Louis Philippe and his forced abdication in 1848; the brief period of the Second Republic and, in 1852, the proclamation of the Second Empire under Napoleon III. Stability was maintained until 1870 when the disasters of the Franco-Prussian War caused the collapse of the government, the deposition of the emperor, the brief and shocking violence of the Paris Commune and, finally, the initiation of the Third Republic.

Across the channel, England's representative government, a constitutional monarchy presided over by the diminutive but iron-willed Victoria, shielded the country against armed insurrection. But the cries from the mills and the mines and the slums grew ever louder and were answered, slowly and grudgingly, by social reform and extended franchise. While the Continent was periodically bathed in blood and unemployment became chronic among European royalty, England emerged as the richest and most stable industrial state of the nineteenth century, a political and economic empire on which the sun never set.

The great International Exhibition of 1851, housed in the Crystal

Palace and sprawled over twenty acres, was an impressive display of England's supremacy and a tribute to the Industrial Revolution. Visitors could view the countless products of British industry and the wonderful machines that produced them—with the help of workingmen, women, and children who put in twelve- to fourteen-hour days. The textile industry had been one of the first to become mechanized. The flying shuttle was introduced as early as 1750, followed by Arkwright's water frame, Hargreave's spinning jenny, Crompton's mule (so called because it was a cross between the jenny and Arkwright's spinner), and finally the power loom. The Jacquard loom, the first machine to be given computerized instructions by punched cards, was in use as early as 1804 and was continually remodeled and improved. The earliest textile mills were water powered; by the 1850 many had been converted to steam. In England alone, the textile industry furnished employment for over one million workers.

Advances were also made in the design of the sewing machine. The first patent was taken out in 1790; a second and equally unsuccessful

The Industrial Revolution brought with it radical advances in the manufacture of textiles and the construction of clothes. Sewing machines now did the work once consigned to legions of seamstresses, and while the final products were less ornate, they were also less costly. The bell-shaped and ground-sweeping dresses in vogue at the time of the Civil War (right) were not yet available ready-made, but the great department stores (left) that were another outgrowth of the Age of Technology furnished all other necessities of a lady's wardrobe.

device was patented in 1829. The first really practical machine was Elias Howe's lockstitch of 1846; new improvements were added by Wilson, Singer, and others. First used for shoemaking, by 1850 the sewing machine was widely employed in the manufacture of ready-made men's wear. By the later 1850's even the great French couturiers used it and by the 1860's, almost all clothing was machine made. Mass production of good, cheap cloth and ready-made clothing required mass distribution. The first department store in Paris, the Ville de France, opened in 1844; it was followed by the Grandes Halles in 1853 and by the Bon Marché in 1876. Similar outlets appeared in England and, eventually, in the United States. As the century progressed, costume—particularly female costume—became ever more involved with the requirements of national economy.

By the early 1850's, men's costume had arrived at the forms it was to retain for the rest of the century. The field was still dominated by English taste with its emphasis on conservatism and careful attention to minute details. As the pace of change in men's wear slowed, this preoccupation with minutiae—the precise height of the collar, the width of the lapel, or the set of a seam—became even more pronounced. Men

had abandoned the gorgeous plumage of the bad old days but they became increasingly finicky about the cut, fit, and general quality of their sober garments. During the later nineteenth century, men were much more particular about this sort of thing than women and, in some measure, they have remained so ever since.

The matched suit consisting of coat, vest, and trousers appeared during the 1850's. At first considered a novelty, by the end of the century it was accepted as the standard masculine uniform. The boxy sack coat (the ancestor of the suit jacket of today) was brought in around 1860. There were other varieties of coats, each intended for specific occasions: frock coats, tail coats, riding coats, shooting coats, and cutaways. The long, heavy overcoat appeared at about the same time and was joined later in the century by the caped Inverness coat.

Men's clothing, with the exception of the shirt and the underwear, was almost entirely restricted to woolen fabrics. Silk was used for linings and occasionally for vests, the last item of men's fashions to retain real dash and elegance. Sober colors were favored; dark blues, browns, greys, and, of course, black. Wild checks and plaids were acceptable for informal wear. Men's costume was apparently designed with two thoughts in mind: first to act as a counterfoil for the brilliant colors and opulent materials of women's fashions and, second, to project an image of unassailable dignity, prosperity and respectability.

Mass production brought respectability within the grasp of all. Men, crowded together at the race track, for example, or in church, or in the business district, would at first glance have seemed indistinguishable and interchangeable. But closer examination would have revealed the inferior fabric and inept cut of factory-produced ready-to-wear garments of the working class and the quality materials and

impeccable fit of the custom-tailored upper classes. The old social distinction between the brocaded aristocrat and the ragged sans-culotte had by no means vanished; it had merely gone underground. The more things change, the more they remain the same.

France continued to dominate women's fashions. In 1845, a feisty, ambitious Englishman, Charles Frederick Worth, settled in Paris as a shop assistant selling textiles, shawls, and ready-made gowns. With an eye for the main chance, he married an equally ambitious shopgirl who became the fashion world's first professional model. He later wormed his way into a partnership with his employer. In 1857, he opened his own couture house at 7 rue de la Paix, and was well on his way to becoming the dictator of the fashion capital of the world. His first important client was Princess de Metternich, who introduced his originals to court where they caught the eye of Eugénie de Montijo, empress to Napoleon III. Worth's fortune was made. The happy combination of a brilliant designer and a beautiful empress gave rise to the stunning fashions that characterized the "Fête Impériale," the heyday of the Second Empire.

By this time women were thoroughly bored with the mousy, middle-class styles of the Louis Philippe era and longed for luxurious, splendid costumes that would serve as a showcase for their own well-fleshed charms. Money was plentiful and society was feverishly active; an almost incessant round of balls, banquets, parties, and receptions required an enormous wardrobe of sensational gowns—morning gowns, walking gowns, riding habits, at-home dresses, town dresses, country dresses, ball gowns, and court costumes. The mills at Lyon were once again turning out exquisite fabrics; sheer organdies, heavy silks, delicate velvets, cashmere, merino, brocade, moiré, taffeta, gauze, mousseline, barège, and tulle. The newly perfected sewing machine

By midcentury the possibilities of crinoline—so beloved by Queen Victoria—had been exhausted. To achieve still greater fullness in women's skirts, dressmakers turned to industry for assistance. The result was cages of muslin, whalebone stays, and steel hoops—and the preposterous silhouette lampooned at left, below. Even tiny children were forced into corsets—small versions of those worn by their elders (left, above)—the better to fit into costumes that were little more than miniature versions of adult clothes (above).

made practical, for the first time, unusually lavish use of both fabric and trimmings. Previously, hand finishing had taken up about ninety percent of the time spent on custom-made gowns; now such elaborate decorations could be applied in a matter of hours rather than days.

The most obvious fashion innovation of the 1850's was the hooped petticoat. Bulky layers of stiff crinoline had already carried skirts to extreme fullness, but the steel hooped cage now bore them out even further and, moreover, allowed the reduction of the number of petticoats which, in turn, decreased the thickness at the waistline. Hoops, so reminiscent of the sixteenth-century farthingale, came in a great variety of styles and shapes. They were often unboned in front to allow greater ease in walking; some were oval to carry the fullness of the gown to the rear; and some were partially collapsible for convenience in sitting. A fashionable lady measured approximately ten yards around at the base, and if two women in a drawing room were company, three were certainly a crowd. Cartoonists had a field day satirizing these grotesque creations. In fact, the style was not funny at all: several women were blown out to sea and drowned; others caught on fire and burned to death, unable to escape from their cages of flaming finery.

The vogue for tight lacing diminished briefly in the 1850's, only to return with greater emphasis in the 1860's. Young ladies were often sewn into their stays by their doting mammas and released only one hour a week for bathing. A thirteen-inch waist was considered ideal although the reality must often have fallen far short. It is a curious fact that of the many splendid dresses that survive from this period, only a very few measure less than twenty inches at the waist.

The costume of the period was openly erotic and, perhaps, auto-erotic as well. Naïve comments in letters and diaries refer to the "delicious sensations" produced by tight lacing. The tiny waists were irresistible above the swaying, bell-shaped skirts that often permitted a tantalizing glimpse of a delicate foot or well-turned ankle. Evening dresses were cut with extreme décolletage; shoulders and bosoms emerged from a froth of the cobweb-fine lace made popular by Eugénie.

The overripe opulence of the period was reflected in its fabrics, colors, and ornament. Velvet was extremely fashionable; light velvet for the evening, heavy, plushlike velvet for day. Colors were rich and even violent, the result of the newly developed analine dyes, and were combined in strong and clashing contrasts. Gowns were encrusted with ornamentation: embroidery, ribbons, lace, galloon, braids, fringes, passementeries, feathers, and artificial flowers. Elaborate heavy jewelry, often copied from ancient Etruscan or Roman models, was a necessity, particularly for evening wear. Great ladies spent fortunes on their wardrobes; women of modest means invested in a sewing machine and pattern books. But all women seemed to dress to the absolute limit of, and even a little beyond, their means. In America, Ralph Waldo Emerson was struck by the remark of a lady who felt that "the sense of being well-dressed gives a feeling of inward tranquillity which religion is powerless to bestow." An anonymous proverb from Eugénie's Spanish homeland puts the obverse case more succinctly: "Only God helps the badly dressed."

The Second Empire did not survive the Franco-Prussian War and the Paris Commune. Neither did the hoop skirt. "The 1870 Revolution is not much in comparison with *my* revolution," crowed Worth; "I dethroned the crinoline!" Worth's genius apparently lay in that he could predict in advance the kind of fashions that would become popular; he introduced new styles before women realized that they were bored with the current modes. He and his sons continued to dominate French couture throughout the rest of the century. With the disappearance of the crinoline, the bustle made its appearance once again. Skirts were bunched up high in the back in a style reminiscent of the later seventeenth century, and both overskirts and underskirts were layered with bouffant ribbons and flounces.

As the decade grew older, the skirt was pulled tighter over the hips, outlining the figure. A new silhouette developed, the skirt smooth and tightly fitted to the hips, then bursting forth in back into a waterfall of pleats, ruffles, flounces, and a long dragging train. Although a great deal of material was used—fourteen yards on the average—the dresses were often so constricted at the hem as to make walking almost impossible. The bustle briefly disappeared and then returned in the middle 1880's in fantastically exaggerated dimensions. New cages were devised that held out the gown at the rear but retained the fashionably flat and narrow front. Tight corseting was still practiced; the bust was thrown upward and out in one vast monolithic surge to balance the padded projection of the derrière. An unsuccessful dress reformer mourned:

The 1850's marked the emergence of the first true house of haute couture—located, as one might expect, in Paris, but headed, a bit unexpectedly, by an Englishman, Charles Frederick Worth. Throughout the remainder of the century Worth dressed the most beautiful and famous women in the world, many of them titled and all of them rich. The peacock-blue silk faille evening gown above came from the famed House of Worth. At right, imitations of the Worth look, complete with bustles, bows, trains, and ruffles.

"Cross the boundaries of any civilized Christian land and you behold a race of gasping, nervous and despairing women who with their compressed hips, torpid lungs, hobbling feet and bilious stomachs apparently consider it their first duty to mortify the flesh."

Toward the end of the century, women were just plain worn out. For decades they had supported a fantastic accumulation of heavy fabrics—pleated, ruffled, flounced, and ruched; they had piled on miles of braid, soutache, passementeries, and ball fringe until they looked like ambulatory versions of their own overcrowded drawing rooms, muffled in velvet draperies and crammed with bibelots, beadwork, wax flowers, peacock feathers, wool work, pampas grass, and classical wreaths lovingly created from the hair of the dear departed. They queened it in society but were denied any other outlet for their talents, any scope for their ambitions. A very few women, through grim determination or economic necessity, had carved careers for themselves in the male dominated world, but the average woman who attempted to look beyond her manifest destiny as wife and mother was, at best, considered eccentric, at worst, dangerously insane, and she was treated accordingly.

But slowly the world was beginning to change. The revolutions of 1870, though not always successful, had spelled the end of immoderate monarchal sentiment and ultra-conservative authoritarianism. Both the fanatic radical and reactionary elements had consumed themselves in political upheavals, and after 1871 Europe as a whole became increasingly democratic. Extended political franchise, greater literacy, improved standards of living, and a sense of the social and economic responsibilities of the state were laying the foundations for the mass democracies of the twentieth century. In this milieu of social and political ferment, women too dared to dream of emancipation. That day was yet far in the future but after the middle 1880's, women rejected the past, deplored the present, and looked to the future.

8

The Democratization of Fashion

During the brief but opulent Edwardian Age, fashion attained new heights of sheer femininity. Opposite, one of the great beauties of the age, Julia Marlowe, wearing one of the most beautiful of turn-of-the-century dresses—a pale nimbus of satin and lace framing alabaster skin and high-piled auburn hair.

ACROSS THE ATLANTIC, far removed from Victoria's England, Eugénie's France, and Worth's world of fashion, a new world power scarcely recovered from the trauma of a civil war was assuming definitive form. The 1870's and 80's in the United States were decades of frantic activity and progress. Vast fortunes were made in oil and steel; commercial empires were founded, and millionaires emerged overnight in banking and industry. The Philadelphia Centennial of 1876 demonstrated the scope of American achievement. Machinery Hall, with a floor plan four times larger than St. Peter's Basilica, was the most impressive of the displays, boldly defining America's industrial progress. Memorial Hall, with its cultural and artistic exhibits, left a great deal to be desired. William Dean Howells was forced to admit: "It is in these things of iron and steel that the national genius most freely speaks. America is voluble in the strong metals and their infinite uses."

With mammon well under control, America courted the muses. Prosperity was avidly pursued but so was gentility. Foremost in the pursuit of the finer things of life was the American woman, relentlessly engaged in the often thankless task of civilizing the aggressive American male. Women dominated social life, trailing their tycoon husbands unobtrusively in their wake. Women ruled the home, firmly and absolutely. It was well that they enjoyed the sovereignty of the hearth; they had precious little opportunity elsewhere.

Just as the man of the family was expected to strive economically onward and upward, so was the lady of the house dedicated to the scaling of ever more glorious social and cultural heights. It was an age of ambition and extreme social mobility, of conscious progress, of conspicuous affluence and equally conspicuous consumption. It was the best of all possible worlds, and anyone who thought otherwise was plainly a fool or an anarchist.

While the men of the decade concealed their rapacity under a sartorial façade of extreme conservatism, their women proclaimed their vaulting social ambitions in costumes of lavish magnificence. In New York, A. T. Stewart's department store, located on "Ladies' Mile," offered behind its cast-iron and plate-glass arcades every luxury for the lady of fashion.

Some articles were ready-made, gloves, for example, or hats, shoes, boots and, of course, lingerie. The corsets of the 1880's were master-

pieces of the engineer's art, crafted—it would appear—from Howell's strong metals. Wire forms were clamped over the bosom and a steel bustle protruded in the rear. The hardware was lashed together with canvas and whalebone, padded with horsehair and stiffened gauze delicately covered with lawn and embellished with lace. Over, around and under this elaborate construction a lady wore cotton or silk stockings, a stocking supporter, a corset cover, a chemise, and three or four petticoats. She might also wear underpants or drawers although these garments were, as yet, far from common and were considered rather racy.

Over all this went the dress. Possibly it was the sudden affluence of the period, or the leisure, or the frenzied scramble for social elevation, but whatever the reason, women's costume was brilliant, gorgeous, and fantastically opulent. Dresses were usually made at home and in many households a seamstress appeared regularly once a week. The sewing machine, now comparatively common, greatly speeded the task, but a great deal of handwork remained. Colors were bold: apple green, peacock green, lapis lazuli, lightning blue, deep red, garnet, cardinal's purple. Fabric was cut lavishly; a carriage dress might require eighteen or twenty yards or more. A variety of fabrics were available; ladies of

The mail-order catalog, an innovation of the last decade of the nineteenth century, introduced high fashion to the hinterlands. By 1897, Sears and Roebuck, the pioneers in the field, were offering a wide variety of dresses at prices as low as $4.50 (near left), a great bargain considering that these full-skirted styles sometimes required eighteen yards of fabric. Also available: "High bust, well-boned, 5 hook spoon, 2 steel corsets of finest Brussels netting" (far left) for the modest sum of 50¢.

modest income relied on wools and cottons, but rich fabrics—brocades, velvets, and silks—were preferred by all who could afford them.

For evening wear, more delicate colors might be chosen. Silks, tulles, brocaded satins in cream, white, pale blues, greens, and yellows were favored. Two colors were always used for important gowns, usually one plain and one patterned, but often two contrasting figures or patterns were chosen. The trim was as opulent as the gown. Bows, laces, ruffles, ruching, and beadwork were applied with a heavy hand. Once such an ensemble was completed and worn in an appropriately stately manner, no one would dare to doubt that he was in the presence of a lady.

This was all very well and good for the women of the major urban centers, but what of the ambitious ladies of the smaller midwestern or southern towns? Unless they had an unusually resourceful general merchant they were doomed to wistful dreams of the world of fashion, a world as yet out of their reach. Unknown to them, help was on the way.

The first mail-order catalogs appeared in the 1890's and brought the material benefits of the Age of Progress to the small towns of America. Necessities and luxuries of every conceivable variety were delivered directly to the door or, at least, to the door of the nearest freight office: soft goods and hard goods, parlor lamps and kitchen ranges, stereoscopes and farm machinery, gasoline engines for father, Haviland china for mother, toys for the children, harnesses for the livestock, and patent medicines for one and all "good for man or beast."

The age of rural isolation was over. Thanks to Sears and Roebuck, the farm wife could follow the fashion trends of the big cities. Styles changed rapidly between 1885 and 1900. The bustle disappeared almost overnight, giving way to the simply styled gored skirt. By contrast, the bodice received more attention. The tight, slim sleeves of the late 1880's puffed out, tentatively at first, and then ballooned into the distinctive leg-of-mutton shape; they grew to astonishing dimensions in mid-decade, then gradually deflated.

The tailored suit was perhaps the most characteristic garment of the era. Made up usually in linen or wool, depending upon the season, it was cut to a simple but elegant pattern. The fabulous wishbooks from the mail-order houses provided them ready-made; an "elegant ladies' suit, made of purple faille, double-breasted jacket, lapels, newest cuffs and sleeves, lined all through with silk taffeta, trimmed with black crochet buttons" might be had for as little as thirteen dollars. The jacket was worn over a shirtwaist "in a choice assortment of new and novel patterns, embracing the season's latest and most choice effects." Collars and often cuffs as well were detachable, and an ordinary blouse could be glorified for a gala evening by the addition of a magnificent silk collar "ornamented with alternating rows of shirred silk and point Venice insertion, very wide lace border all around."

Ready-to-wear garments were convenient, but home sewing was still the rule rather than the exception. In mail-order catalogs of the 1890's, almost twice as many pages were devoted to fabric than to ladies' ready-made garments. Wash goods ran from 4½¢ to 16¢ a yard, silks from 25¢ to 90¢, free samples upon request. The colors and printed figures of both the yard goods and the finished articles were generally conservative, more businesslike, one might say, more appropriate for the active and adventuresome New Woman.

For quietly, demurely and without excessive fanfare, a new woman was emerging. Comparatively few years had made a great deal of difference. Education for women was now readily available, more acceptable, and of increasingly higher quality. More women worked, for the new inventions and the expanding economy provided wider employment. And, perhaps most significant of all, decent women now engaged in sports.

Roller skating, golf, lawn tennis, and bicycling—these were the great female emancipators of the Gay Nineties. Bicycling was particularly liberating. Young women became more mobile as they tore around the countryside in generally unchaperoned groups, relying upon their numbers for their safety. Furthermore, they tore around in pants suits. The bicycling costume of the 1890's was highly decorous: a tailored long-skirted coat, knickers, leather or cloth gaiters, and a boyish cap. Women finally had an acceptable excuse to don the reform garments that Mrs. Amelia Bloomer had unsuccessfully promoted back in the 1850's. Conservative males were horrified and cited dire passages from Leviticus. The costume was denounced by pulpit, press, and politicians for its immodesty. As usual, to no avail.

The twentieth century was ushered in at last, hailed variously as the Age of Optimism, the Age of Confidence and, curiously, as the Age of Innocence. The optimism and the confidence, at least, could not be challenged. As an Age of Innocence, it was perhaps best represented by the ladies, particularly as personified in the character of the Gibson Girl. In the flesh this ideal was approached by Maude Adams, Ethel Barrymore, or Alice Roosevelt Longworth, the President's spirited daughter. To many, "Princess Alice" embodied the ideal concept of American womanhood even if she did smoke in public, which is more than Mr. Gibson's girls were allowed to do.

Fashions were elegant and intensely feminine. Women adopted a swanlike silhouette and dresses fell into a graceful S-curve, somewhat reminiscent of the last gasp of Art Nouveau. Fluid lines, eccentric curves, drooping forms, and chalky, pastel colors characterized the costume and decor of the period. Not the least eccentric of the curves were those induced by the corsets; they practically dislocated the spine, throwing the hips back and the bust forward. Rustproof models were available for the newly acceptable fad of sea bathing.

Tailored suits and crisp shirtwaist outfits were still popular, but many young women began to favor the lingerie dress, a softly fitted costume derived from the tea gown of the previous decade. These delicate frocks were sewn in light wash fabrics—voile, organdy, batiste, lawn, cambric, or dimity in white, off-white, or pale pastels. Wide tucks and pin tucks shaped the material softly. Lace sleeves, inserts, and bands of embroidery added to the artistic effect.

Mail-order houses carried the new modes to the hinterlands. A really elegant lingerie dress with Valenciennes lace insertion could be had from Sears in 1908 for around $10.00. Slightly less ornate examples

An ample figure, upswept hair, and a demure demeanor—these were the attributes of the Gibson Girl (below). Illustrator Charles Dana Gibson's principal models were the three Langhorne sisters, one of whom eventually became Lady Astor, but his actual subject was the Ideal American Woman. The female virtues associated with his drawings were often attached, in the public imagination, to well-known women of the day, among them the actresses Minnie Maddern Fiske and Ethel Barrymore (right).

CHARLES
FROHMAN
PRESENTS

ETHEL BARRYMORE

averaged around $6.00. All the other delicate necessities were also available: the Armorside abdominal corset at $1.25, fabulous petticoats dripping with embroidery and lace for less than a dollar, and corset covers —hemstitched, laced, ribboned, ruffled and beaded—for about 50¢.

To top the costume off there were hats! Pages and pages of fantastic hats were presented, swimming in silk roses, violets, beaded medallions, cherries, grapes, ostrich plumes, aigrettes—whipped together with crushed velvet, shirred silk, Chantilly lace, taffeta ribbon, and yards of chiffon veiling.

The outward appearance was one of exquisite elegance and of refined femininity carried almost to the point of utter helplessness. Appearances were never more deceptive. As the decade grew to a close, women were becoming more involved than ever before in major public interests. The American woman campaigned for temperance, equal rights, and female suffrage. She was active, vocal, and determined. And when events of the following decade provided her with the opportunity, she was quick to seize it, leaving the bell jar of Victorian propriety to take her place as an equal in the world of men.

In America, the aggressive confidence and optimism of the early 1900's began to wilt during the following decade. Extreme labor unrest forced the conclusion that this, after all, was not necessarily the best of all possible worlds. The formerly comfortable policy of isolation cracked and splintered as America was drawn increasingly deeper into European conflicts.

In 1917, America formally entered into World War I. Over ten million young men registered for the draft, and as they were gradually enlisted and shipped off to camp, their places at home were filled by women. Previously, it had been an obvious abomination for women to work at men's jobs; now it was an equally obvious patriotic duty. Women were emancipated. Formal political recognition of his fact was yet to come. American women did not receive suffrage until 1920 but, to all practical intents and purposes, from the middle of the decade they were free agents.

Nowhere was this emancipation reflected more clearly than in the world of fashion. Many of the jobs newly opened to women required men's clothing and women could—and did—wear overalls or even aviator's breeches without shame and censure. Led by Alice Longworth, America's women gratefully donated their steel corsets to the war effort, thereby releasing—according to the War Industries Board—28,000 tons of steel, enough to build two battleships.

Part Gibson Girl and part suffragette; part doting daughter, part imperious reformer— Alice Roosevelt Longworth was in many ways the very model of the restless American woman, chafing against the constraints of pre-World War I society. At left, a photograph of "Princess Alice" on her wedding day in 1906. She stands in the East Room of the White House, her long train stretched before her, her famous father on her left and her husband on her right.

Under the sanctifying excuse of wartime austerity, women dressed more sensibly. Skirts began inching up to the background counterpoint of thunderous denunciations from the pulpit. The female form reassumed its natural outlines and, for the first time in over a century, it became possible once again for women to move and breathe freely.

While the dress reform of this decade would never have been achieved without the liberating influence of the war years, the general trends had been introduced into fashion in a fairly conventional manner around 1910. The designer ultimately responsible for the new modes was the Frenchman Paul Poiret. Intrigued by the costumes of the Near and Far East, he drew most of his inspiration from these sources. He initiated corsetry reform, relaxed the waist, and moved the bust back to its natural habitat. Skirts were narrowed and eventually shrank into the tight hobble skirt. A long tunic was worn over the underskirt; gradually it became fuller and shorter and gently draped at the hips.

By 1914 the dominant characteristic of female costume was the lampshade silhouette; a full flaring tunic over a narrow skirt. When World War I broke out, patriotic austerity caused no immediate change in fashion until women began to be recruited for the home front as substitutes for the absent men. The tight underskirt was an obvious hindrance to their new way of life. The logical solution was to drop the tunic to below the calf and omit the underskirt entirely. Women had achieved short skirts.

During the war years, clothes were decorous and understated. Shepherd checks in black and white were popular, chiefly on account of their quiet, unobtrusive attractiveness. There was, after all, no point in drawing undue attention to the emancipation of women. Women's dresses and suits relied mainly on box pleats for both shaping and decoration, with applied trim restricted to the collars and cuffs. High fashion went in for more flamboyant attire: lustrous satins, silks, and velvets, draped tulle overskirts, and lavish fur trim. But as the war ended and the twenties approached, a new factor emerged in American costume. The entire concept of high fashion was redefined and democratized, brought within the reach of all. This trend had been intermittently apparent since the 1890's, but by 1920 Americans had become the best-dressed people in the world. European journalists commented upon the attractive and modestly priced costumes, the benefits of mass production, which—outwardly at least—erased social distinctions.

The Roaring Twenties: historical research has yet to discover just how or when that nickname was first applied. It might well have been derived from the nationwide bellow that ascended to the heavens on October 28, 1920, when the National Prohibition Act became the law of the land. Of course, the decade had its serious aspects, but things great and serious were swallowed up in the pervasive carnival atmosphere. Open materialism and unabashed hedonism ushered in "the greatest, gaudiest spree in history." Encouraged and often initiated by the first nationwide exploitation of mass media, fads sprang up overnight and expired just as rapidly. The flapper, her antics immortalized in the cartoons of John Held Jr., was the heroine of the age. Short-haired, short-skirted, with turned-down hose and rouged knees, escorted by a college boy with slicked-down hair, raccoon coat, and Oxford bags, she must have seemed to her mother, the gentle Gibson Girl, like a creature from outer space.

The movies provided the major entertainment of the day; movie stars were idolized and their lives—both on and off the silver screen—furnished impossibly glamourous models for popular emulation. The other chief amusement of the era appears to have been the studied evasion of the restrictions of the Volstead Act, with humorous side effects upon the world of fashion. The hip flask was an indispensable accessory for a fashionable gentleman—or lady. Canes and walking sticks were carried by both sexes; often hollow, they concealed a handy jolt. Russian boots were suddenly popular, presumably because the wide tops could conceal a pint bottle or two. All in all, the era provided unbounded opportunities for the exercise of American ingenuity.

The modes of the period were practically dictated by Coco Chanel. She introduced the simple, understated look of the tweed suit, cardigan jacket, jersey blouse, and the single string of pearls. Bobbed hair was due largely to her influence, as was the abandonment of the corset in favor of a bust bodice or brassiere, which flattened the figure into submission. The waist as well as the bust disappeared, and the slim, gently flared skirts began migrating upward.

The new styles flattered an entirely new age group. Edwardian fashions had favored mature, regal ladies who had the wherewithal to fill the majestically proportioned corsets. In the twenties, the tubular, sexless dresses suited the tubular, sexless figure. Older women steamed, dieted, and exercised—all, it would appear, to no avail. In the photographs of the era, the young, gawky girls have the appeal of a pasture full of colts; mature women look like badly tied sacks of potatoes.

The trend peaked around 1926. The hem reached the knee, the waistline dropped down as if to meet it and, in evening wear, the décolletage—both in front and in back—slithered toward the waist. While Chanel had popularized simple and natural materials such as jersey, which had formerly served only for the Englishman's balbriggan underwear, exotic fabrics were favored for late afternoon and evening: light gauzes, transparent silks and chiffons, georgettes, Shantungs, crepes, and voiles appeared, lavished with sequins, beads, and feathers.

Religious leaders fulminated against these styles and, after the initial flush had worn off, the textile and fashion industries joined in the general imprecations. The new modes used very little material and their extreme simplicity of design encouraged home sewing. The industries took a direct stand in an attempt to revive long skirts, but with little immediate success. Eventually the skirt started moving back down by itself; in the later twenties hems were again below the calf in much the same location that they had occupied in 1915. The belt crept up to its natural position. For evening wear, the frontal décolletage became more modest although the southern exposure remained extreme.

Then came the crash. At the end of the decade the bottom dropped out of the stock market and the frenetic gaiety of the twenties was blotted out in the grim reality of the Great Depression. The 1930's have often been called the inevitable hangover following the binge of

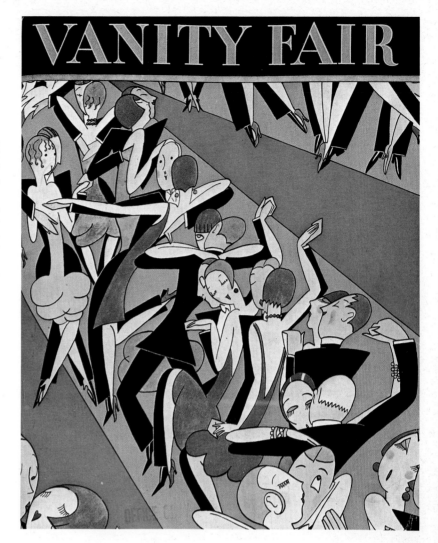

The principal legacy of the Jazz Age was not the bare knee and even barer back, hallmarks of the flappers who grace the cover of this 1927 issue of Vanity Fair, *but an emphasis on youthful looks that still dominates the world of high fashion. The heyday of the mature woman was over, possibly forever; haute couture belonged to skinny girls with bright eyes, bobbed hair, and boundless energy.*

the previous decade. Unemployment rose to an all-time high; wages fell to a level of bare subsistence. Bread lines and soup kitchens were set up in all major cities, and Hoovervilles mushroomed in vacant lots and on the outskirts of towns, meager shelter for thousands of homeless. In 1933, with the inauguration of Roosevelt and his New Deal, the economy began to revive. But even with prosperity just around the corner, the nation's celebration was brief, muted, and low-keyed, for the decade that had opened with the Depression closed under the fearful shadow of world war.

Basically the 1930's marked a period of austerity. Personal freedom among the young was taken for granted but infrequently flaunted and seldom abused. Drinking became legal again and, as night must follow day, was considerably less attractive. College life was more serious; undoubtedly there were still flappers manqué, but their places were rapidly being filled by earnest young students of sociology and economics. The blatant sexuality of the twenties was considerably subdued; the feminine ideal was now the wholesome girl next door or the fallen angel, just slightly tarnished and worn around the edges.

Fashion had its ups and downs in the decade, particularly in regard to skirt length. As if in warning, in 1929, just before the crash, skirts suddenly went down, down, and down. In the early thirties fashion came to a standstill. Hand-me-downs had always been the rule of the day among thrifty families; now they became almost fashionable. Children scarcely knew what it was to have new store-bought clothing, as harried mothers labored to cut down and remake adult garments that had become hopelessly outmoded or outworn. Depression babies had layettes sewn from sugar sacks; school children often wore underwear embellished with the trademarks of Pillsbury's or Robin Hood flour.

During the Depression, classic suits and dresses came into their own. Garments had to last and classics emphasized good quality and conservative styles. Even among the well-to-do it was chic to boast of wearing the same gown for several seasons. Sensible tailored suits were highly favored. Worn with a neat, white blouse they became the distinctive attire of the office worker, the college girl, and the young society matron alike.

The shirtwaist dress was another enduring classic to emerge from this era. An all-purpose garment, a good shirtwaist could be—and usually was—worn for all occasions except for the most formal. Long or short sleeved, they usually had modest necklines and skirts well below the knee. Alas for the rouged patellae of the twenties; that portion of the anatomy was now considered almost obscene. The bust was rounded but not emphasized, and the waistline, indicated by a belt or a sash, was in its normal position. Pockets, both real and simulated, were used for decoration and buttons marched down the front, up the back or around the sides in veritable regiments. A few bows never hurt anything either. Dresses often appeared with a coordinated coat, usually of contrasting fabric and color, but lined with the dress fabric. The short, boxy coat was seen everywhere, cut with wide lapels, wide shoulders, and a profusion of the inevitable pockets. The overall effect was one of sensibility, modesty, and a generally no-nonsense attitude toward life. The sensational bias-cut evening gowns of the era, clinging like a second skin, might well have told another story, but during the daylight hours, the image was that of Miss Apple Pie, the girl next door.

In 1940, many Americans attempted to ignore the cloud of war that hung thickly over Europe. After Pearl Harbor, such an attitude was no longer possible. America armed and mobilized in haste. Wartime austerity was immediately reflected in the world of fashion. The Wartime Production Board, under Directive L85, restricted the manufacture of clothing. Hems could be only two inches deep, only one pocket was permitted per blouse, no skirt could be more than seventy-two inches around at the hem, and ruffles were forbidden altogether. Dresses were short; hemlines rose and leveled off just below the knee. The look was feminine, but it was a determined sort of feminism. The shoulder line had masculine overtones; daytime clothing was unusually mannish with shoulder pads that would have done justice to a linebacker.

During the war, fashion was not taken very seriously. Skirts, blouses, and sweaters were worn by all females from eight to eighty. Women again filled the home-front work force. That perennial favorite, the tailored suit, dominated the white-collar world, while slacks and

One of the giants of twentieth century fashion was Paul Poirot, who created a new, uncorseted style that emphasized the natural lines of the body. His designs, inspired by the work of Bakst and Benois for the Ballets Russes, featured vivid colors and Oriental elements such as harem pants and wide kimono sleeves. Above, a Poirot ensemble; at right, a Mandarin coat created by one of Poirot's better-known colleagues, Dœuillet.

jeans ruled in industry. Cut off from the fashion source at Paris—which was in an equal state of paralysis—America was forced to improvise and turned to the military for inspiration. Eisenhower jackets, Montgomery berets, and other patriotic motifs were common. Chinese and Russian themes came and went in direct relation to the political climate. Evening wear, predictably, was unusually alluring. Whether white, bouffant, and innocent, or black, sequined, and slinky, it served the same fascinating purpose and contributed, in no small measure, to the baby boom of the mid-1940's.

After the war, fashion dithered around until 1947 when Dior's New Look was unveiled as a stylish and elegant release from wartime restrictions. Skirts dropped to just above the ankle, expanded into incredible yardages, and were worn over petticoats stiff with crinoline and heavy with flounces of lace. Alternatively, the skirt might be tight at the hem, almost as restrictive as the hobble skirt of pre-World War I, but draped and pouffed at the hips or worn with a full tunic. Either way, fabric was used lavishly. The waistline was forced to forego the casual sloppiness of wartime and was carefully defined under tight jackets or bodices. Corsetry revived in the merry widow or other waist nippers, which trimmed inches off the middle and redistributed the surplus in supposedly less conspicuous areas. The wired strapless bra, often padded, took care of the bust. The fashionable woman of the late forties was almost as heavily armor-plated as her grandmother at the turn of the century.

Shoulder pads were out. Perhaps no single article of fashion ever looked so archaic in such a short time. Shoulders were rounded, as was the bust; the waist was improbably narrow; the hips were occasionally padded, and the legs hidden under yards of fabric. And such fabric—silks, taffetas, failles, and moirés in dark, subdued colors for afternoon and evening or delicate shades of aquamarine, powder blue, ice blue, and soft pinks and yellows for the day. Shoes, high-heeled and dainty with ankle straps and open toes, were worn over sheer dark or color-coordinated nylons. Small, frivolous hats were worn and make-up was used heavily. The overall effect was distinctly feminine.

The neo-Edwardian style of the New Look prevailed, in modified forms, for approximately a decade. It was graceful and appealing and, after the initial shock had worn off, women fell in love with it, waist nippers and all. Well, perhaps not all women. "I adore you," Chanel commented to Dior, "but you dress women like armchairs."

Another phenomenon that emerged from the mid-forties was the cult of the teen-ager. Somewhere along the way, perhaps during the war years when most men were in the service and many women on the assembly line, teen-agers emerged into the spotlight, both socially and economically. They have been there ever since. Suddenly, teens were supposed to be more responsible; after all, they could no longer be dismissed as mere children when another year, perhaps two, might take their generation to Normandy or the South Pacific. Certainly they had money to spend. Youth magazines, pioneered by *Seventeen*, flooded the market. Teen fashions, such as Minx Modes or Jonathan Logan, appealed to the junior miss and her elder sister as well. The fashion industries had suddenly discovered a new and highly lucrative market.

From the mid-forties on, the American teen-agers built their own subculture, an intricate pattern of fads, slang, and customs that evolved and mutated at the speed of light. And, rapidly as the merchandisers sought the teen-age dollar, the teens usually stayed several jumps ahead. The blue-jean fad began in the forties, no one knows how or why. But thousands of high school and college girls blossomed forth in baggy blue jeans, rolled to the knee, worn with a man's shirt several sizes too large, with the shirttails flapping in the breeze.

The Edwardian delicacy of the New Look partially civilized the young savages and got them back, temporarily, into skirts. Throughout most of the fifties, the school uniform consisted of a pleated wool skirt, usually a plaid, worn well below the knee, topped off with a matching or color-coordinated sweater set. The bras worn under the sweaters were rigidly conical in shape, padded, wired, and unnaturally uplifted. A silk scarf or pearls at the neckline and saddle shoes and bobby sox below completed the costume. But even the teen-agers, like their older sisters and their mothers, remained faithful throughout the fifties to modifications of the New Look for more elegant and formal attire.

The sack dress and its variations were introduced in 1958. The basic element of the design was the eased sheath which, from its simple outlines, soon sprouted loose back panels and a low-slung beltline. It could be belted in the general area of the mid-thigh for a bag shape or bunched into a pouf with a constricted hem. The wilder variations died a quick and merciful death; skirts began creeping up once again, the belt was dropped entirely and the basic straight shift emerged. Throughout the Western world parquet flooring, antique rugs and, no

doubt, countless male feet still bear the scars of another fashion trend of the period—the stiletto heel.

By the late fifties fashion did not seem to know where it was going, but neither did anything—or anyone—else. The super-technologies born of the war had not solved all the problems of the troubled world, quite the contrary. Atomic jitters were hard to live with and the arms race and the space race were no less uncomfortable. The Beat Generation produced its own life styles and its own poets, disillusioned dropouts from the American dream of peace, prosperity, and conformity for all.

Only one world suits the 1960's: psychedelic. It was a decade of action, violence, protest, experiment, and counterculture. Above all, it was a period of youth. The Kennedy administration encouraged youthful involvement in movements such as Vista, Aspira, and the Peace Corps. But the optimism soured and was replaced by the shattered illusions and the abrasive hostility of young revolutionaries.

The tendency to drop out of society continued. Hippies followed the beatniks of the fifties, and were themselves superseded by the flower children who, in turn were displaced by the street people. To flaunt their rejection of society, they created their own fashions, scruffy, scroungy, ultra-casual styles worn in direct and deliberate defiance of their horrified elders. They understood quite well that costume expresses the deepest values of society and that to reject the one was to attack the other. By the end of the decade, these rebels and misfits were to exert considerable influence on the world of fashion.

The sixties opened with the basic and simple A-line dress, evolved by Courrèges from the Dior shift of the late fifties. Skirts began moving up again, and up, and up. The mini skirt bared most of the thigh, and the micro-mini bared practically everything else. Both were worn over panti-hose in wild colors and exotic knits and patterns. Boots, in all lengths, completed the look. Brilliant Pucci prints—both the real thing and many imitations—were seen everywhere, as were vinyls, stretch jerseys, and fake furs. Legs were the focal point of the fashions, but while hips and bosoms were relatively unimportant, they were not corseted out of existence. Indeed, corsetry had gone by the board altogether, and many young women had also discarded their bras.

Besides the normal progressive trends, fashion also showed a preoccupation with fantasy. Thrift shops were ransacked for costumes of the twenties, thirties, and forties. Boutiques promoted exotic foreign outfits: kaftans, djellabas, kurtas, sheepskin coats from Afghanistan, embroidered robes from Greece, and boldly patterned dashikis from Africa. Young women and, to a lesser extent, young men as well, acted out their fantasies appearing variously as Indian maids, gypsy princesses, Edwardian dandies, pioneer couples in granny gowns and jeans, Bonnie and Clyde, or Dr. Zhivago and Lara.

Mini, micro, midi, or maxi—the skirt controversy was all very interesting but the most significant development of the late sixties was the emergence of the pants suit. Women had attempted pants since the dear dead days of the sainted Mrs. Bloomer. Chanel, in the 1930's, made them acceptable as sportswear and during the war years overalls and jeans were a practical necessity. But trousers for women always had decided overtones of the resort or the assembly line. They had never been totally respectable.

Culottes were introduced in the late sixties to the heartfelt relief of mothers who were growing grey from watching their teeny-bopper daughters bend over. Then, suddenly, the tailored pants suit was everywhere, chic, elegant, and convenient. And comfortable. Only the woman who has frozen through a winter or two with the southern half of her anatomy hanging out of a mini skirt can truly appreciate the comfort of pants. Just when it seemed that the pants suit might fade away with other crazy fads of the decade, Paris introduced the longuette or midi skirt. Not entirely delighted by the look and faced with the dilemma of not knowing which way the hem was going to jump, women climbed back into their pants and from this secure retreat looked on while the midi all but expired after one brief season.

Fashion in the 1970's lost its rigidity and became extremely flexible. Indeed, it is more accurate to speak of life styles rather than of fashion as such. Almost everyone, but the young people especially, dressed to identify with the life styles of their preference. This revolution in dress originated with the young and relatively poor—the hippies, flower children, and street people—and percolated upward into higher society. Social adaptability provided a great deal of sartorial leeway. A neatly shorn junior executive in a brokerage house could don a long, shaggy wig to make the scene Saturday night in Greenwich Village. Conversely, a budding rock musician might invest in a short wig to avoid hassles at school, home, or office. Bare feet and filthy, faded blue jeans might well be seen emerging from an expensive sports car, or the ubiquitous grey flannel suit might be observed on a motor bike.

Women's fashions were limited only by the personality of the wearer and, to an extent, by her age bracket. Older women who had already lived through the forties or the fifties were unlikely to feel any

nostalgic desire to revisit them. In general, it was the women of this age group who appeared most receptive to the new Paris styles. The streets, department stores, and singles bars of any major American city today reveal an astonishing variety of costumes. A few gypsy princesses are still around rubbing shoulders with Persian nomads. Micro skirts that barely cover the behind converse amiably with granny gowns. Worn, frayed, and friendly jeans (possibly purchased in that condition at considerable expense) exchange views with hot pants.

Men also exhibit more variation in their costume. Ultraconservatives still adhere to the grey flannel suits made famous in the fifties and corporation men and bankers seldom venture out of their pinstripes, but increasingly men's clothing is becoming richer, more colorful, and more inventive. As with women's costumes, many aspects of men's fashions have also worked their way up from the subcultures. High heels

The diversity of contemporary fashion is exemplified by two of its most successful present-day practitioners: Yves Saint Laurent (above), whose recent collections have emphasized opulent fabrics and—for the "Beyond Fantasy" wedding costumes shown here—a surfeit of glittering accessories; and Halston (right), whose name has become synonymous with extreme elegance and simplicity of design.

Flexibility is the keynote of fashion in the seventies. More often than not, style has come from the streets—a reflection of liberated lifestyles and idiosyncratic tastes exemplified by the ubiquitous denims seen opposite. Some designer clothes have aped these trends, but the best of them (opposite page) have focused instead on classical materials, good tailoring, and flattering lines.

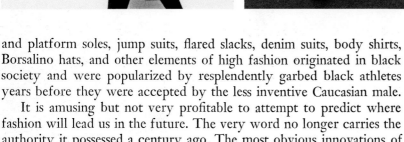

and platform soles, jump suits, flared slacks, denim suits, body shirts, Borsalino hats, and other elements of high fashion originated in black society and were popularized by resplendently garbed black athletes years before they were accepted by the less inventive Caucasian male.

It is amusing but not very profitable to attempt to predict where fashion will lead us in the future. The very word no longer carries the authority it possessed a century ago. The most obvious innovations of twentieth-century fashion are the introduction of short skirts and pants for women and a gradual return to more splendid clothing for men; but even more important is the greater freedom, individuality, and inventiveness of costume. Fashion, once a tyrant, has become almost a friend.

Future fashions could perhaps be defined if future society could be defined. The twentieth century has evolved problems that can no

longer be solved by existing formulas. Former patterns of history shrink before the grim giants of the present—population and mechanization.

A third giant, the pace of change itself, is equally grim. In the past, significant social and technological changes evolved slowly; man had time to adjust from generation unto generation. Today and tomorrow, the frenetic pace, even more than the changes themselves, may induce severe psychological trauma. Future shock, as it has so aptly been labeled, is now feared more than the future itself. Fashions will almost certainly continue to change rapidly, and almost certainly they will continue to encourage individualism. The toughest and most durable part of the human psyche is the ego, desperately struggling for recognition of its uniqueness. In the future as in the past, fashion will continue to project identity, giving the ego outward form and meaning.

VOGUE

SUMME
PLANS

The Black an
White Ide

The Linen Li

Transparer
Fashion

Incorporating Vanity Fair
April 1, 1950
Price 50 Cents

IN A LITERARY FASHION

"Beware of any enterprise that requires new clothes," Henry David Thoreau warned readers of Walden *in 1854, and since then many have doubtless needed his eminently sensible advice. But clothes are an integral part of virtually every human enterprise, whether new or old, and consequently they have assumed an important symbolic function in world literature. There, as never in real life, clothes and clothes alone can truly make the man. They can suggest his character, forecast his behavior, and even govern his destiny. The seventeenth-century English poet Robert Herrick understood all this when he dubbed this brief verse "Upon Julia's Clothes":*

> *When as in silks my Julia goes,*
> *Then, then (me thinks) how sweetly flowes*
> *That liquefaction of her clothes.*
> *Next, when I cast mine eyes and see*
> *That brave Vibration each way free;*
> *O how that glittering taketh me!*

The following survey of costume in literature begins, not illogically, with John Milton's lines describing mankind's first garment, a girdle of fig leaves. In this excerpt from Paradise Lost, *Adam and Eve are first encountered clad in nothing save their "native honor."*

Two of far nobler shape erect and tall,
God-like erect, with native honor clad
In naked majesty seemed lords of all,
And worthy seemed, for in their looks divine
The image of their glorious Maker shone,
Truth, wisdom, sanctitude severe and pure,
Severe but in truth filial freedom placed;
Whence true authority in men; though both
Not equal, as their sex not equal seemed;
For contemplation he and valor formed,
For softness she and sweet attractive grace;
He for God only, she for God in him.
His fair large front and eye sublime declared
Absolute rule; and hyacinthine locks
Round from his parted forelock manly hung
Clust'ring, but not beneath his shoulders broad:
She as a veil down to the slender waist
Her unadorned golden tresses wore
Disheveled, but in wanton ringlets waved
As the vine curls her tendrils, which implied
Subjection, but required with gentle sway,
And by her yielded, by him best received,
Yielded with coy submission, modest pride,
And sweet reluctant amorous delay.

1900

Nor those mysterious parts were then concealed;
Then was not guilty shame; dishonest shame
Of Nature's works, honor dishonorable,
Sin-bred, how have ye troubled all mankind
With shows instead, mere shows of seeming pure,
And banished from man's life his happiest life,
Simplicity and spotless innocence.
So passed they naked on, nor shunned the sight
Of God or angel, for they thought no ill;
So hand in hand they passed, the loveliest pair
That ever since in love's embraces met,
Adam the goodliest man of men since born
His sons, the fairest of her daughters Eve. . . .

. . . Silent, and in face
Confounded, long they sat, as strucken mute,
Till Adam, though not less than Eve abashed,
At length gave utterance to these words constrained:
   'O Eve, in evil hour thou didst give ear
To that false worm, of whomsoever taught
To counterfeit man's voice, true in our fall,
False in our promised rising; since our eyes
Opened we find indeed, and find we know
Both good and evil, good lost and evil got,
Bad fruit of knowledge, if this be to know,
Which leaves us naked thus, of honor void,
Of innocence, of faith, of purity,
Our wonted ornaments now soiled and stained,
And in our faces evident the signs
Of foul concupiscence; whence evil store,
Even shame, the last of evils; of the first
Be sure then. How shall I behold the face
Henceforth of God or angel, erst with joy
And rapture so oft beheld? Those heav'nly shapes
Will dazzle now this earthly, with their blaze
Insufferably bright. O might I here
In solitude live savage, in some glade
Obscured, where highest woods impenetrable
To star or sunlight, spread their umbrage broad
And brown as evening! Cover me, ye pines,
Ye cedars, with innumerable boughs
Hide me, where I may never see them more.
But let us now, as in bad plight, devise
What best may for the present serve to hide
The parts of each from other that seem most
To shame obnoxious, and unseemliest seen,
Some tree whose broad smooth leaves together sewed,

And girded on our loins, may cover round
Those middle parts, that this newcomer, Shame,
There sit not, and reproach us as unclean."
    So counseled he, and both together went
Into the thickest wood; there soon they chose
The fig-tree, not that kind for fruit renowned,
But such as at this day to Indians known
In Malabar or Deccan spreads her arms
Branching so broad and long, that in the ground
The bended twigs take root, and daughters grow
About the mother tree, a pillared shade
High overarched, and echoing walks between;
There oft the Indian herdsman shunning heat
Shelters in cool, and tends his pasturing herds
At loop-holes cut through thickest shade. Those leaves
They gathered, broad as Amazonian targe,
And with what skill they had, together sewed,
To gird their waist, vain covering if to hide
Their guilt and dreaded shame, O how unlike
To that first naked glory!

JOHN MILTON
Paradise Lost, 1667

The Iliad, *the first half of Homer's epic account of the Trojan War and its tragic aftermath, recounts the adventures of Agamemnon, king of Mycenae, husband of Clytemnestra, and leader of the Greek forces that lay siege to Troy. In this passage the warrior-monarch dons his battle dress—breastplate and sword, shield and helmet—while his troops prepare to set sail for Ilium.*

And King Agamemnon
Shouted commands for the Argives to dress for battle,
And he himself put on the gleaming bronze.
First he covered his shins with greaves, fair greaves
With angle-clasps of silver. Next, about his chest,
He put the breastplate given to him by Cinyras,
King of Cyprus. For he had heard the wide-spread
News that Achaeans were soon to set sail for Troy,
And so had graciously sent the breastplate for King
Agamemnon to wear and enjoy. Inlaid upon it
Were ten dark bands of blue lapis, twelve of gold,
And twenty of shining tin, and three blue-lapis
Serpents arched up toward the neck on either side,
Like the rainbows that Cronos' son hangs in the clouds as signs
For mortal men. And about his shoulders he slung
His sword, flashing with studs and straps of gold

1910

And sheathed in a silver scabbard. Then he took up
His warlike, richly wrought shield, man-covering and splendid
To see. For inlaid upon it were ten bright circles
Of bronze and twenty bosses of shining tin
Surrounding a central boss of blue lapis. And set
In the lapis, the awesome head of the Gorgon glared grimly
Forth, flanked by the figures of Panic and Rout.
From this great shield hung a baldric of glittering silver
Whereon a blue-lapis, three-headed serpent writhed.
And on his head he put a helmet, four-horned
And double-crested, with plume of horsehair defiantly
Waving above him. He also took up two sturdy
Spears, keenly pointed with bronze, and far up into
The sky the bright bronze flashed. And now, to honor
The King of golden Mycenae, Athena and Hera
Thundered.

HOMER
The Iliad, c. 500 B.C.

The French physician and author François Rabelais has lent his own surname to the brand of ribald humor and biting social satire that characterizes his best-known works, Gargantua *and* Pantagruel, *which were published in five installments between 1532 and 1564. The enduring popularity of the former work, based upon a collection of familiar anecdotes concerning a legendary local giant, has provided the language with another neologism—"gargantuan," meaning of prodigious size. In a chapter entitled "How They Apparelled Gargantua," Rabelais outlines the dilemma faced by the tailors charged with the awesome task of outfitting the young giant.*

Being of this age, his father ordained to have clothes made to him in his own livery, which was white and blue. To work then went the tailors, and with great expedition were clothes made, cut and sewed, according to the fashion that was then in request. I find by the ancient records or pancarts, to be seen in the chamber of accounts, or Court of the Exchequer, at Montsoreau, that he was accoutred in manner as followeth. To make him every shirt of his were taken up nine hundred ells [meters] of Chateleraud linen, and two hundred for the gussets, in manner of cushions, which they put under his arm-pits. His shirt was not gathered nor plaited, for the plaiting of shirts was not found out till the seamstresses (when the point of their needle was broken) began to work and occupy with the tail. There were taken up for his doublet, eight hundred and thirteen ells of white satin, and his points fifteen hundred and nine dogs' skins and a half. . . .

For his breeches were taken up eleven hundred and five ells and a third of white broad-cloth. They were cut in the form of pillars, chamfered, channelled, and pinked behind, that they might not overheat his reins; and were, within the panes, puffed out with the lining of as much blue damask as was needful; and remark, that he had very good leg-harness, proportionable to the rest of his stature.

For his codpiece were used sixteen ells and a quarter of the same cloth, and it was fashioned on the top like unto a [flying buttress] most gallantly fastened with two enamelled clasps, in each of which was set a great emerald, as big as an orange; for, as says Orpheus, lib. de lapidibus, and Plinius, libro ultimo, it hath an erective virtue and comfort and comfortative of the natural member. The exiture, out-jecting or out-standing of his codpiece, was of the length of a yard, jagged and pinked, and withal bagging, and strutting out with the blue damask lining, after the manner of his breeches. But had you seen the fair embroidery of the small needlework pearl, and the curiously interlaced knots, by the gold-smith's art set out and trimmed with rich diamonds, precious rubies, fine torquoises, costly emeralds, and Persian pearls, you would have compared it to a fair Cornucopia, or horn of abundance, such as you see in antiques, or as Rhea gave to the two nymphs, Amalthea and Ida, the nurses of Jupiter.

And, like to that horn of abundance, it was still gallant, succulent, droppy, sappy, pithy, lively, always flourishing, always fructifying, full of juice, full of flower, full of fruit, and all manner of delight. I avow God, it would have done one good to have seen him, but I will tell you more of him in the book which I have made of the Dignity of Cod-pieces. One thing I will tell you, that, as it was both long and large, so was it well furnished and victualled within, nothing like unto the hypo-critical codpieces of some fond wooers, and wench-courters, which are stuffed only with wind, to the great prejudice of the female sex.

For his shoes were taken up four hundred and six ells of blue crimson velvet, and were very neatly cut by parallel lines, joined in uniform cylinders. For the soling of them were made use of eleven hundred hides of brown cows, shapen like the tail of a keeling.

For his coat were taken up eighteen hundred ells of blue velvet, dyed in grain, embroidered in its borders with fair gilliflowers, in the middle decked with silver pearl, intermixed with plates of gold, and stores of pearls, hereby showing, that in his time he would prove an especial good fellow, and singular whip-can.

His girdle was made of three hundred ells and a half of silken serge, half white and half blue, if I mistake it not. His sword was not of Val-entia, nor his dagger of Saragossa, for his father could not endure these hidalgos borrachos maranisados como diablos: but he had a fair sword made of wood, and the dagger of boiled leather, as well painted and gilded as any man could wish.

His purse was made of the cod of an elephant, which was given him by Her Pracontal, proconsul of Lybia.

FRANCOIS RABELAIS
Gargantua, 1532-64

VOGUE

JANUARY 1, 1915
PRICE 25 CENTS

1915

Charles Dickens, who gave popular English literature the quintessential waif, Little Nell, and the pluckiest of preadolescent heroes, David Copperfield, also created the most famous of all jilted brides, Miss Havisham. In the opening chapter of Great Expectations, *young Pip is sent to visit Estella, Miss Havisham's cheeky ward. After a discomfiting encounter with Estella outside the gates of the gloomy old house, Pip is led inside for his first audience with the mansion's aged mistress.*

We went into the house by a side door—the great front entrance had two chains across it outside—and the first thing I noticed was, that the passages were all dark, and that she had left a candle burning there. She took it up, and we went through more passages and up a staircase, and still it was all dark, and only the candle lighted us.

At last we came to the door of a room, and she said, "Go in."

I answered, more in shyness than politeness, "After you, miss."

To this, she returned: "Don't be ridiculous, boy; I am not going in." And scornfully walked away, and—what was worse—took the candle with her.

This was very uncomfortable, and I was half afraid. However, the only thing to be done being to knock at the door, I knocked, and was told from within to enter. I entered, therefore, and found myself in a pretty large room, well lighted with wax candles. No glimpse of daylight was to be seen in it. It was a dressing-room, as I supposed from the furniture, though much of it was of forms and uses then quite unknown to me. But prominent in it was a draped table with a gilded looking-glass, and that I made out at first sight to be a fine lady's dressing-table.

Whether I should have made out this object so soon, if there had been no fine lady sitting at it, I cannot say. In an arm-chair, with an elbow resting on the table and her head leaning on that hand, sat the strangest lady I have ever seen, or shall ever see.

She was dressed in rich materials—satins, and lace, and silks—all of white. Her shoes were white. And she had a long white veil dependent from her hair, and she had bridal flowers in her hair, but her hair was white. Some bright jewels sparkled on her neck and on her hands, and some other jewels lay sparkling on the table. Dresses less splendid than the dress she wore, and half-packed trunks, were scattered about. She had not quite finished dressing, for she had but one shoe on—the other was on the table near her hand—her veil was but half arranged, her watch and chain were not put on, and some lace for her bosom lay with those trinkets, and with her handkerchief, and gloves, and flowers, and a Prayer-book, all confusedly heaped about the looking-glass.

It was not in the first few moments that I saw all these things, though I saw more of them in the first moments than might be supposed. But, I saw that everything within my view which ought to be white, had been white long ago, and had lost its lustre, and was faded and yellow. I saw that the bride within the bridal dress had withered like the dress, and like the flowers, and had no brightness left but the brightness of her sunken eyes. I saw that the dress had been put upon the rounded figure of a young woman, and that the figure upon which it now hung loose, had shrunk to skin and bone. Once, I had been taken to see some ghastly waxwork at the Fair, representing I know not what impossible personage lying in state. Once, I had been taken to one of our old marsh churches to see a skeleton in the ashes of a rich dress, that had been dug out of a vault under the church pavement. Now, waxwork and skeleton seemed to have dark eyes that moved and looked at me. I should have cried out, if I could.

"Who is it?" said the lady at the table.

"Pip, ma'am."

"Pip?"

"Mr. Pumblechook's boy, ma'am. Come—to play."

"Come nearer; let me look at you. Come close."

It was when I stood before her, avoiding her eyes, that I took note of the surrounding objects in details, and saw that her watch had stopped at twenty minutes to nine, and that a clock in the room had stopped at twenty minutes to nine.

"Look at me," said Miss Havisham. "You are not afraid of a woman who has never seen the sun since you were born?"

I regret to state that I was not afraid of telling the enormous lie comprehended in the answer "No."

"Do you know what I touch here?" she said, laying her hands, one upon the other, on her left side.

"Yes, ma'am." (It made me think of the young man.)

"What do I touch?"

"Your heart."

"Broken!"

She uttered the word with an eager look, and with strong emphasis, and with a weird smile that had a kind of boast in it. Afterwards, she kept her hands there for a little while, and slowly took them away as if they were heavy.

"I am tired," said Miss Havisham. "I want diversion, and I have done with men and women. Play."

I think it will be conceded by my most disputatious reader, that she could hardly have directed an unfortunate boy to do anything in the wide world more difficult to be done under the circumstances.

"I sometimes have sick fancies," she went on, "and I have a sick fancy that I want to see some play. There, there!" with an impatient movement of the fingers of her right hand; "play, play, play!"

For a moment, with the fear of my sister's working me before my eyes, I had a desperate idea of starting round the room in the assumed character of Mr. Pumblechook's chaise-cart. But, I felt myself so unequal to the performance that I gave it up, and stood looking at Miss Havisham in what I supposed she took for a dogged manner, inasmuch as she said, when we had taken a good look at each other:

VOGUE April 17·1920 Price 35 cts

The Vogue Company

1920

"Are you sullen and obstinate?"

"No, ma'am, I am very sorry for you, and very sorry I can't play just now. If you complain of me I shall get into trouble with my sister, so I would do it if I could; but it's so new here, and so strange, and so fine—and melancholy—" I stopped, fearing I might say too much, or had already said it, and we took another look at each other.

Before she spoke again, she turned her eyes from me, and looked at the dress she wore, and at the dressing-table, and finally at herself in the looking-glass.

"So new to him," she muttered; "so old to me; so strange to him, so familiar to me; so melancholy to both of us! Call Estella."

As she was still looking at the reflection of herself, I though she was still talking to herself, and kept quiet

"Call Estella," she repeated, flashing a look at me. "You can do that. Call Estella. At the door."

To stand in the dark in a mysterious passage of an unknown house, bawling Estella to a scornful young lady neither visible nor responsive, and feeling it a dreadful liberty so to roar out her name, was almost as bad as playing to order. But, she answered at last, and her light came along the dark passage like a star.

Miss Havisham beckoned her to come close, and took up a jewel from the table, and tried its effect upon her fair young bosom and against her pretty brown hair. "Your own, one day, my dear, and you will use it well. Let me see you play cards with this boy."

"With this boy! Why, he is a common labouring-boy!"

I thought I overheard Miss Havisham answer—only it seemed so unlikely—"Well? You can break his heart."

CHARLES DICKENS
Great Expectations, 1861

Antony and Cleopatra is a tale of national calamity as well as personal tragedy, for the wayward passions that engulf the adulterous Roman triumvir and the amorous Egyptian queen inevitably bring disaster to their empires. William Shakespeare's description of the lovers' initial meeting limns Cleopatra with the bold strokes befitting a great monarch and renowned beauty, portraying her as a perfect union of royal pomp and ravishing femininity.

MAECENAS She's a most triumphant lady, if report be square to her.

ENOBARBUS When she first met Mark Antony, she pursed up his heart upon the river of Cydnus.

AGRIPPA There she appeared indeed, or my reporter devised well for her.

ENOBARBUS

I will tell you.

The barge she sat in, like a burnished throne,

Burned on the water. The poop was beaten gold;
Purple the sails, and so perfuméd that
The winds were lovesick with them; the oars were silver,
Which to the tune of flutes kept stroke and made
The water which they beat to follow faster,
As amorous of their strokes. For her own person,
It beggared all description. She did lie
In her pavilion, cloth-of-gold of tissue,
O'erpicturing that Venus where we see
The fancy outwork nature. On each side her
Stood pretty dimpled boys, like smiling Cupids,
With divers-coloured fans, whose wind did seem
To glow the delicate cheeks which they did cool,
And what they undid did.

AGRIPPA   O, rare for Antony!

ENOBARBUS

Her gentlewomen, like the Nereides,
So many mermaids, tended her i' th' eyes,
And made their bends adornings. At the helm
A seeming mermaid steers. The silken tackle
Swell with the touches of those flower-soft hands
That yarely frame the office. From the barge
A strange invisible perfume hits the sense
Of the adjacent wharfs. The city cast
Her people out upon her; and Antony,
Enthroned i' th' market-place, did sit alone,
Whistling to th' air; which, but for vacancy,
Had gone to gaze on Cleopatra too,
And made a gap in nature.

AGRIPPA   Rare Egyptian!

WILLIAM SHAKESPEARE
The Tragedy of Antony and Cleopatra, 1607•

*The most famous piece of needlework in American history is un-
doubtedly Betsy Ross's flag, but Hester Prynne's handiwork must run a
close second. Confined to the Salem, Massachusetts, stockade on a
charge of adultery, the heroine of Nathaniel Hawthorne's 1850 master-
piece,* The Scarlet Letter, *embroiders a red A upon the bodice of her
dress in accordance with what the author calls "the whole dismal severity of the Puritanic code of law."*

The door of the jail being flung open from within, there appeared, in
the first place, like a black shadow emerging into sunshine, the grim and
grisly presence of the town-beadle, with a sword by his side, and his
staff of office in his hand. This personage prefigured and represented in
his aspect the whole dismal severity of the Puritanic code of law,

1925

which it was his business to administer in its final and closest application to the offender. Stretching forth the official staff in his left hand, he laid his right upon the shoulder of a young woman, whom he thus drew forward; until, on the threshold of the prison-door, she repelled him, by an action marked with natural dignity and force of character, and stepped into the open air, as if by her own free will. She bore in her arms a child, a baby of some three months old, who winked and turned aside its little face from the too vivid light of day; because its existence, heretofore, had brought it acquainted only with the gray twilight of a dungeon, or other darksome apartment of the prison.

When the young woman—the mother of this child—stood fully revealed before the crowd, it seemed to be her first impulse to clasp the infant closely to her bosom; not so much by an impulse of motherly affection, as that she might thereby conceal a certain token, which was wrought or fastened into her dress. In a moment, however, wisely judging that one token of her shame would but poorly serve to hide another, she took the baby on her arm, and, with a burning blush, and yet a haughty smile, and a glance that would not be abashed, looked around at her townspeople and neighbors. On the breast of her gown, in fine red cloth, surrounded with an elaborate embroidery and fantastic flourishes of gold thread, appeared the letter A. It was so artistically done, and with so much fertility and gorgeous luxuriance of fancy, that it had all the effect of a last and fitting decoration to the apparel which she wore; and which was of a splendor in accordance with the taste of the age, but greatly beyond what was allowed by the sumptuary regulations of the colony.

The young woman was tall, with a figure of perfect elegance on a large scale. She had dark and abundant hair, so glossy that it threw off the sunshine with a gleam, and a face which, besides being beautiful from regularity of feature and richness of complexion, had the impressiveness belonging to a marked brow and deep black eyes. She was ladylike, too, after the manner of the feminine gentility of those days; characterized by a certain state and dignity, rather than by the delicate, evanescent, and indescribable grace, which is now recognized as its indication. And never had Hester Prynne appeared more lady-like, in the antique interpretation of the term, than as she issued from the prison. Those who had before known her, and had expected to behold her dimmed and obscured by a disastrous cloud, were astonished, and even startled, to perceive how her beauty shone out, and made a halo of the misfortune and ignominy in which she was enveloped. It may be true, that, to a sensitive observer, there was something exquisitely painful in it. Her attire, which, indeed, she had wrought for the occasion, in prison, and had modelled much after her own fancy, seemed to express the attitude of her spirit, the desperate recklessness of her mood, by its wild and picturesque peculiarity. But the point which drew all eyes, and, as it were, transfigured the wearer—so that both men and women, who had been familiarly acquainted with Hester Prynne, were now impressed as if they beheld her for the first time—was that SCARLET LETTER, so fantastically embroidered and illuminated upon her bosom. It had the effect of a spell, taking her out of the ordinary relations with humanity, and enclosing her in a sphere by herself.

"She hath good skill at her needle, that's certain," remarked one of her female spectators; "but did ever a woman, before this brazen hussy, contrive such a way of showing it! Why, gossips, what is it but to laugh in the faces of our godly magistrates, and make a pride out of what they, worthy gentlemen, meant for a punishment?"

"It were well," muttered the most iron-visaged of the old dames, "if we stripped Madam Hester's rich gown off her dainty shoulders; and as for the red letter, which she hath stitched so curiously, I'll bestow a rag of mine own rheumatic flannel, to make a fitter one!"

"O, peace neighbors, peace!" whispered their youngest companion; "do not let her hear you! Not a stitch in that embroidered letter, but she has felt it in her heart."

The grim beadle now made a gesture with his staff.

"Make way, good people, make way, in the King's name!" cried he. "Open a passage; and, I promise ye, Mistress Prynne shall be set where man, woman and child, may have a fair sight of her brave apparel, from this time till an hour past meridian. A blessing on the righteous Colony of the Massachusetts, where iniquity is dragged out into the sunshine! Come along, Madam Hester, and show your scarlet letter in the market-place!"

NATHANIEL HAWTHORNE
The Scarlet Letter, 1850

James Fenimore Cooper is said to have taken up writing on a dare. Having boasted to his wife that he could write a better book than the one he was reading at the time, he found himself challenged to do so. Over the next two decades Cooper wrote a dozen novels, among them the interrelated series known as the Leatherstocking tales, stories of the American wilderness that won him widespread popular and critical acclaim, both at home and abroad. The most perfectly plotted of these tales is The Deerslayer, *in which Cooper introduces "a man of gigantic mould" who is in every respect the archtypal frontier hero, right down to his buckskins.*

"Here is room to breathe in!" exclaimed the liberated forester, as soon as he found himself under a clear sky, shaking his huge frame like a mastiff that has just escaped from a snowbank. "Hurrah! Deerslayer; here is daylight, at last, and yonder is the lake."

These words were scarcely uttered when the second forester dashed aside the bushes of the swamp, and appeared in the area. After making a hurried· adjustment of his arms and disordered dress, he joined his companion, who had already begun his disposition for a halt.

1930

"Do you know this spot?" demanded the one called Deerslayer, "or do you shout at the sight of the sun?"

"Both, lad, both; I know the spot, and am not sorry to see so useful a fri'nd as the sun. Now we have got the p'ints of the compass in our minds once more, and 'twill be our own faults if we let anything turn them topsy-turvy ag'in, as has just happened. My name is not Hurry Harry, if this be not the very spot where the land hunters 'camped the last summer, and passed a week. See! yonder are the dead bushes of their bower, and here is the spring. Much as I like the sun, boy, I've no occasion for it to tell me it is noon; this stomach of mine is as good a timepiece as is to be found in the colony, and it already p'ints to half-past twelve. So open the wallet, and let us wind up for another six hours' run."

At this suggestion, both set themselves about making the preparations necessary for their usual frugal but hearty meal. We will profit by this pause in the discourse to give the reader some idea of the appearance of the men, each of whom is destined to enact no insignificant part in our legend. It would not have been easy to find a more noble specimen of vigorous manhood than was offered in the person of him who called himself Hurry Harry. His real name was Henry March; but the frontiersmen having caught the practice of giving *sobriquets* from the Indians, the appellation of Hurry was far oftener applied to him than his proper designation, and not unfrequently he was termed Hurry Skurry, a nickname he had obtained from a dashing, reckless, offhand manner, and a physical restlessness that kept him so constantly on the move, as to cause him to be known along the whole line of scattered habitations that lay between the province and the Canadas. The stature of Hurry Harry exceeded six feet four, and being unusually well proportioned, his strength fully realized the idea created by his gigantic frame. The face did not discredit to the rest of the man, for it was both good-humored and handsome. His air was free, and though his manner necessarily partook of the rudeness of a border life, the grandeur that pervaded so noble a physique prevented it from becoming altogether vulgar.

Deerslayer, as Hurry called his companion, was a very different person in appearance, as well as in character. In stature he stood about six feet in his moccasins, but his frame was comparatively light and slender, showing muscles, however, that promised unusual agility, if not unusual strength. His face would have had little to recommend it except youth, were it not for an expression that seldom failed to win upon those who had leisure to examine it, and to yield to the feeling of confidence it created. This expression was simply that of guileless truth, sustained by an earnestness of purpose, and a sincerity of feeling, that rendered it remarkable. At times this air of integrity seemed to be so simple as to awaken the suspicion of a want of the usual means to discriminate between artifice and truth; but few came in serious contact with the man, without losing this distrust. . . .

Both these frontiersmen were still young, Hurry having reached the age of six or eight and twenty, while Deerslayer was several years his junior. Their attire needs no particular description, though it may be well to add that it was composed in no small degree of dressed deer-skins, and had the usual signs of belonging to those who pass their time between the skirts of civilized society and the boundless forests. There was, notwithstanding, some attention to smartness and the picturesque in the arrangements of Deerslayer's dress, more particularly in the part connected with his arms and accoutrements. His rifle was in perfect condition, the handle of his hunting knife was neatly carved, his powder horn was ornamented with suitable devices lightly cut into the material, and his shot pouch was decorated with wampum. On the other hand, Hurry Harry, either from constitutional recklessness, or from a secret consciousness how little his appearance required artificial aids, wore everything in a careless, slovenly manner, as if he felt a noble scorn for the trifling accessories of dress and ornaments. Perhaps the peculiar effect of his fine form and great stature was increased rather than lessened, by this unstudied and disdainful air of indifference.

JAMES FENIMORE COOPER
The Deerslayer, 1841

Venice at the turn of the century was the most international of cities, its Lido hotels frequented by well-heeled travelers from such distant European capitals as Oslo, London, and Moscow. It is hardly surprising, therefore, that Gustav von Aschenbach, the protagonist of Thomas Mann's famed novella, Death in Venice, *should encounter a family of elegantly attired Polish aristocrats in the dining room of his hotel. What is exceptional is the intensity of Aschenbach's Platonic attraction to the youngest member of that family, a frail boy named Tadzio.*

A solitary, unused to speaking of what he sees and feels, has mental experiences which are at once more intense and less articulate than those of a gregarious man. They are sluggish, yet more wayward, and never without a melancholy tinge. Sights and impressions which others brush aside with a glance, a light comment, a smile, occupy him more than their due; they sink silently in, they take on meaning, they become experience, emotion, adventure. Solitude gives birth to the original in us, to beauty unfamiliar and perilous—to poetry. But also, it gives birth to the opposite: to the perverse, the illicit, the absurd. Thus the traveller's mind still dwelt with disquiet on the episodes of his journey hither: on the horrible old fop with his drivel about a mistress, on the outlaw boatman and his lost tip. They did not offend his reason, they hardly afforded food for thought; yet they seemed by their very nature fundamentally strange, and thereby vaguely disquieting. Yet here was the sea; even in the midst of such thoughts he saluted it with his eyes, exulting that Venice was near and accessible. At length he turned round,

1935

disposed his personal belongings and made certain arrangements with the chambermaid for his comfort, washed up, and was conveyed to the ground floor by the green-uniformed Swiss who ran the lift.

He took tea on the terrace facing the sea and afterwards went down and walked some distance along the shore promenade in the direction of Hôtel Excelsior. When he came back it seemed to be time to change for dinner. He did so, slowly and methodically as his way was, for he was accustomed to work while he dressed; but even so found himself a little early when he entered the hall, where a large number of guests had collected—strangers to each other and affecting mutual indifference, yet united in expectancy of the meal. He picked up a paper, sat down in a leather armchair, and took stock of the company, which compared most favourably with that he had just left.

This was a broad and tolerant atmosphere, of wide horizons. Subdued voices were speaking most of the principal European tongues. That uniform of civilization, the conventional evening dress, gave outward conformity to the varied types. There were long, dry Americans, large-familied Russians, English ladies, German children with French *bonnes*. The Slavic element predominated, it seemed. In Aschenbach's neighbourhood Polish was being spoken.

Round a wicker table next him was gathered a group of young folk in charge of a governess or companion—three young girls, perhaps fifteen to seventeen years old, and a long-haired boy of about fourteen. Aschenbach noticed with astonishment the lad's perfect beauty. His face recalled the noblest moment of Greek sculpture—pale, with a sweet reserve, with clustering honey-coloured ringlets, the brow and nose descending in one line, the winning mouth, the expression of pure and godlike serenity. Yet with all this chaste perfection of form it was of such unique personal charm that the observer thought he had never seen, either in nature or art, anything so utterly happy and consummate. What struck him further was the strange contrast the group afforded, a difference in educational method, so to speak, shown in the way the brother and sisters were clothed and treated. The girls, the eldest of whom was practically grown up, were dressed with an almost disfiguring austerity. All three wore half-length slate-coloured frocks of cloister-like plainness, arbitrarily unbecoming in cut, with white turn-over collars as their only adornment. Every grace of outline was wilfully suppressed; their hair lay smoothly plastered to their heads, giving them a vacant expression, like a nun's. All this could only be by the mother's orders; but there was no trace of the same pedagogic serverity in the case of the boy. Tenderness and softness, it was plain, conditioned his existence. No scissors had been put to the lovely hair that (like the Spinnario's) curled about his brows, above his ears, longer still in the neck. He wore an English sailor suit, with quilted sleeves that narrowed round the delicate wrists of his long and slender though still childish hands. And this suit, with its breast-knot, lacings, and embroideries, lent the slight figure something "rich and strange," a spoilt, exquisite air. The observer saw him in half profile, with one foot in its black patent leather advanced, one elbow resting on the arm of his basket-chair, the cheek nestled into the closed hand in a pose of easy grace, quite unlike the stiff subservient mien which was evidently habitual to his sisters. Was he delicate? His facial tint was ivory-white against the golden darkness of his clustering locks. Or was he simply a pampered darling, the object of a self-willed and partial love? Aschenbach inclined to think the latter. For in almost every artist nature is inborn a wanton and treacherous proneness to side with the beauty that breaks hearts, to single out aristocratic pretensions and pay them homage.

A waiter announced, in English, that dinner was served. Gradually the company dispersed through the glass doors into the dining-room. Late-comers entered from the vestibule or the lifts. Inside, dinner was being served; but the young Poles still sat and waited about their wicker table. Aschenbach felt comfortable in his deep arm-chair, he enjoyed the beauty before his eyes, he waited with them.

The governess, a short, stout, red-faced person, at length gave the signal. With lifted brows she pushed back her chair and made a bow to the tall woman, dressed in palest grey, who now entered the hall. This lady's abundant jewels were pearls, her manner was cool and measured; the fashion of her gown and the arrangement of her lightly powdered hair had the simplicity prescribed in certain circles whose piety and aristocracy are equally marked. She might have been, in Germany, the wife of some high official. But there was something faintly fabulous, after all, in her appearance, though lent it solely by the pearls she wore: they were well-nigh priceless, and consisted of earrings and a three-stranded necklace, very long, with gems the size of cherries.

The brother and sisters had risen briskly. They bowed over their mother's hand to kiss it, she turning away from them, with a slight smile on her face, which was carefully preserved but rather sharp-nosed and worn. She addressed a few words in French to the governess, then moved towards the glass door. The children followed, the girls in order of age, then the governess, and last the boy. He chanced to turn before he crossed the threshold, and as there was no one else in the room, his strange, twilit grey eyes met Aschenbach's, as our traveller sat there with the paper on his knee, absorbed in looking after the group.

There was nothing singular, of course, in what he had seen. They had not gone in to dinner before their mother, they had waited, given her a respectful salute, and but observed the right and proper forms on entering the room. Yet they had done all this so expressly, with such self-respecting dignity, discipline, and sense of duty that Aschenbach was impressed. He lingered still a few minutes, then he, too, went into the dining-room, where he was shown a table far off the Polish family, as he noted at once, with a stirring of regret.

THOMAS MANN
Death in Venice, 1912

1940

Madame Bovary, *the story of a sentimental spendthrift suffocated by her bourgeois existence, created a scandal in France upon its publication in 1856. Its author, Gustave Flaubert, was even prosecuted for immorality, but he and his adulterous heroine were ultimately acquitted. This description of the romantic Emma Rouault's wedding to stolid, sensible Charles Bovary—a steady accretion of precisely observed details—typifies Flaubert's flawless style.*

The guests arrived betimes, in all sorts of conveyances—one-horse tilt-carts, waggonettes, old cabriolets minus their hoods, carriers' vans with leather curtains. The young folk from the villages close by drove up in farm carts, standing up in rows, holding on to the side rails to prevent themselves from falling, jolting along at a short, sharp trot. Some of the people came from thirty miles away, from such places as Goderville, Normanville and Cany. All the relations on both sides had been invited. Old quarrels had been patched up, and letters sent to friends they had not heard of for ages.

From time to time the crack of a whip was heard the other side of the hedge. Then the gate would swing open, and a cart would enter. It would drive at a canter right up to the doorstep, pull up with a jerk and discharge its occupants, who would clamber down on either side, rubbing the stiffness out of their knees and stretching their arms. The ladies, in their best bonnets, wore town-made costumes, gold watch-chains, tippets with ends crossing over at the waist, or little coloured kerchiefs fastened behind with a pin and showing a little bit of neck at the back. The little boys, dressed like their papas, seemed rather ill at ease in their new clothes (a good few of them were sporting the first pair of boots they had ever had in their lives), and alongside of them, not daring to utter a word, and wearing her white first communion dress lengthened for the occasion, you might see a gawky girl of anything from fourteen to sixteen—a sister or a cousin, no doubt—all red and flustered, her hair plastered down with strong-smelling pomade and terribly afraid of soiling her gloves. As there were not enough stable-boys to unharness all the horses, the gentlemen rolled up their sleeves and turned-to themselves. According to their different social grades they wore dress-coats, frock-coats, jackets, and cardigans—fine black suits, venerable symbols of family respectability which only issued from the press on occasions of special solemnity; frock-coats with voluminous skirts floating in the wind, collars like cylinders and pockets as big as sacks; coats of coarse homespun, of the sort usually worn with a cap with a band of copper round the peak; very short jackets with two buttons in the small of the back, close together like a pair of eyes, the abbreviated tails of which looked as if they had been cut out of a single block with a carpenter's chisel. Yet others (but they, for sure, would have to sit below the salt) were wearing their party smocks, that is to say, smocks with the collar turned down over the shoulder, the back gathered in with little puckers, and encircled, very low down, by an embroidered belt.

And the shirts bulged out on the chests like breastplates. All the gentlemen had had their hair cut, their ears were sticking out from their heads, and they had all shaved especially close. . . .

The Mairie being but a mile or so from the farm they went on foot, and as soon as the ceremony at the church was over they trudged back again. The procession, at first keeping well together, resembled a coloured scarf as it undulated through the countryside, winding slowly along the narrow footpath through the green cornfields. But before long it began to straggle, and broke up into separate groups that loitered on the way to gossip. The fiddler went on ahead, the top of his fiddle all bedecked with streamers; after him walked the bridegroom and his bride, the relations and friends following in what order they pleased. Last of all came the children, who amused themselves by plucking little sprays of oats, or had a little game all to themselves, when no one was looking. Emma's dress, which was too long for her, dragged a little behind. Every now and again she would stop to gather it up and, delicately, with her gloved hand, pick off the blades of rough grass and bits of briar, while Charles stood sheepishly by, waiting till she had finished. Farmer Rouault, resplendent in a new silk hat, the cuffs of his best coat covering his hands as far as his finger-tips, had given his arm to the dowager Madame Bovary. Monsieur Bovary senior, who in his heart thought all these people very small beer indeed, had come in an austere frock-coat of military cut with a single row of buttons. He was delivering himself of some rather dubious jocularities to a fair-haired country wench, who curtseyed, and blushed, and didn't know what to say. The rest of the party talked business or indulged in a little skylarking by way of warming themselves up for the gaiety to come; and whenever you cared to listen, you could hear the scrape-scrape of the fiddler who pranced on ahead, fiddling over hill and dale. When he noticed that the party had fallen a good way behind, he stopped to take breath and applied the rosin with vigour to his bow, so that the strings should squeak the louder. Then he marched on again, swaying the top of his instrument alternately up and down, the better to mark the time. The sound of the fiddle startled the birds far and wide.

The table had been laid under the roof of the cartshed. Upon it there stood four sirloins, six dishes of hashed chicken, stewed veal, three legs of mutton and, in the centre, a comely roast sucking-pig flanked with four hogs-puddings garnished with sorrel. At each corner was a decanter filled with spirits. Sweet cider in bottles was fizzling out round the corks, and every glass had already been charged with wine to the brim. Yellow custard in great dishes, which would undulate at the slightest jog of the table, displayed on its smooth surface the initials of the wedded pair in arabesques of candied peel. They had had recourse to a confectioner at Yvetot for the tarts and the iced cakes. As he was just starting business in the district, he had

1945

given a special eye to things; and when the dessert was brought on, he himself, personally, carried in a set piece which drew cries of admiration from the assembled company. At the base of this erection was a rectangular piece of blue cardboard, representing a temple with porticoes, colonnades, and stucco statuettes all around in little niches embellished with gilt-paper stars. Above it, on the second storey, stood a castle-keep or donjon wrought in Savoy cake, surrounded with diminutive fortifications in angelica, almonds, raisins, and bits of orange; and finally, on the topmost level of all, which was nothing less than a verdant meadow where there were rocks with pools of jam and boats made out of nut-shells, was seen a little Cupid balancing himself on a chocolate swing, the posts of which were tipped with two real rosebuds. . . .

Two days after the wedding, the newly married couple departed. Charles could not be away from his practice any longer. Farmer Rouault sent them home in his carriage, and went with them himself as far as Vassonville. There he kissed his daughter "good-bye," stepped down from the carriage and started for home again. When he had gone about a hundred paces he halted, and gazing at the carriage vanishing into the distance, its wheels turning in the dust, he heaved a profound sigh. Then he thought of his own wedding, of the days gone by, of his wife's first pregnancy. He, too, was very happy when he took her from her father's, back to his own house; when she rode behind him on the crupper, trotting through the snow; for the season was near Christmas and the country all white. One of her arms was holding on to him, and on the other she carried her basket. The wind fluttered the long lace strings of her Caux head-dress and sometimes blew them across her mouth, and when he turned his head he saw close by him, just above his shoulder, her little rosy mouth smiling beneath the gold rim of her bonnet. To warm her fingers she would thrust them, every now and again, into his bosom. How far away it seemed now, all that!

GUSTAVE FLAUBERT
Madame Bovary, 1856

F. Scott Fitzgerald's requiem for the Jazz Age, The Great Gatsby, *is a sharp but not unsympathetic portrait of the ersatz glamour, cultural sterility, and pervasive ennui that seemed to envelop American high society in the years immediately following World War I. It chronicles the spectacular rise and equally spectacular fall of Jay Gatz, who amasses a huge illicit fortune in the mistaken assumption that vast wealth will win him what breeding never could—the hand of Daisy Buchanan, a woman he has long adored from afar. The first encounter between Daisy and Gatsby, as he now calls himself, occurs not at his feudal mansion overlooking Long Island Sound but in the adjacent cottage of Nick Carraway, their go-between and Fitzgerald's narrator.*

The day ageed upon was pouring rain. At eleven o'clock a man in a raincoat, dragging a lawn-mower, tapped at my front door and said that Mr. Gatsby had sent him over to cut my grass. This reminded me that I had forgotten to tell my Finn to come back, so I drove into West Egg Village to search for her among soggy whitewashed alleys and to buy some cups and lemons and flowers.

The flowers were unnecessary, for at two o'clock a greenhouse arrived from Gatsby's, with innumerable receptacles to contain it. An hour later the front door opened nervously, and Gatsby, in a white flannel suit, silver shirt, and gold-colored tie, hurried in. He was pale, and there were dark signs of sleeplessness beneath his eyes.

"Is everything all right?" he asked immediately.

"The grass looks fine, if that's what you mean."

"What grass?" he inquired blankly. "Oh, the grass in the yard." He looked out the window at it, but, judging from his expression, I don't believe he saw a thing.

"Looks very good," he remarked vaguely. "One of the papers said they thought the rain would stop about four. I think it was *The Journal*. Have you got everything you need in the shape of—of tea?"

I took him into the pantry, where he looked a little reproachfully at the Finn. Together we scrutinized the twelve lemon cakes from the delicatessen shop.

"Will they do?" I asked.

"Of course, of course! They're fine!" and he added hollowly, ". . . old sport."

The rain cooled about half-past three to a damp mist, through which occasional thin drops swam like dew. Gatsby looked with vacant eyes through a copy of Clay's *Economics*, starting at the Finnish tread that shook the kitchen floor, and peering toward the bleared windows from time to time as if a series of invisible but alarming happenings were taking place outside. Finally he got up and informed me, in an uncertain voice, that he was going home.

"Why's that?"

"Nobody's coming to tea. It's too late!" He looked at his watch as if there was some pressing demand on his time elsewhere. "I can't wait all day."

"Don't be silly; it's just two minutes to four."

He sat down miserably, as if I had pushed him, and simultaneously there was the sound of a motor turning into my lane. We both jumped up, and, a little harrowed myself, I went out into the yard.

Under the dripping bare lilac-trees a large open car was coming up the drive. It stopped. Daisy's face, tipped sideways beneath a three-cornered lavender hat, looked out at me with a bright ecstatic smile.

"Is this absolutely where you live, my dearest one?"

The exhilarating ripple of her voice was a wild tonic in the rain. I had to follow the sound of it for a moment, up and down, with my ear alone, before any words came through. A damp streak of hair lay

like a dash of blue paint across her cheek, and her hand was wet with glistening drops as I took it to help her from the car.

"Are you in love with me," she said low in my ear, "or why did I have to come alone?"

"That's the secret of Castle Rackrent. Tell your chauffeur to go far away and spend an hour."

"Come back in an hour, Ferdie." Then in a grave murmur: "His name is Ferdie."

"Does the gasoline affect his nose?"

"I don't think so," she said innocently. "Why?"

We went in. To my overwhelming surprise the living-room was deserted.

"Well, that's funny," I exclaimed.

"What's funny?"

She turned her head as there was a light dignified knocking at the front door. I went out and opened it. Gatsby, pale as death, with his hands plunged like weights in his coat pockets, was standing in a puddle of water glaring tragically into my eyes.

With his hands still in his coat pockets he stalked by me into the hall, turned sharply as if he were on a wire, and disappeared into the living-room. It wasn't a bit funny. Aware of the loud beating of my own heart I pulled the door to against the increasing rain.

For half a minute there wasn't a sound. Then from the living-room I heard a sort of choking murmur and part of a laugh, followed by Daisy's voice on a clear artificial note:

"I certainly am awfully glad to see you again."

A pause; it endured horribly. I had nothing to do in the hall, so I went into the room.

Gatsby, his hands still in his pockets, was reclining against the mantelpiece in a strained counterfeit of perfect ease, even of boredom. His head leaned back so far that it rested against the face of a defunct mantelpiece clock, and from this position his distraught eyes stared down at Daisy, who was sitting, frightened but graceful, on the edge of a stiff chair.

"We've met before," muttered Gatsby. His eyes glanced momentarily at me, and his lips parted with an abortive attempt at a laugh. Luckily the clock took this moment to tilt dangerously at the pressure of his head, whereupon he turned and caught it with trembling fingers and set it back in place. Then he sat down, rigidly, his elbow on the arm of the sofa and his chin in his hand. . . .

Tea is served, the rain abates, and the threesome adjourns to Gatsby's enormous house, which stands nearby.

Instead of taking the short cut along the Sound we went down to the road and entered by the big postern. With enchanting murmurs Daisy admired this aspect or that of the feudal silhouette against the sky, admired the gardens, the sparkling odor of jonquils and the frothy odor of hawthorn and plum blossoms and the pale gold odor of kiss-me-at-the-gate. It was strange to reach the marble steps and find no stir of bright dresses in and out of the door, and hear no sound but bird voices in the trees.

And inside, as we wandered through Marie Antoinette music-rooms and Restoration salons, I felt that there were guests concealed behind every couch and table, under orders to be breathlessly silent until we had passed through. As Gatsby closed the door of "the Merton College Library" I could have sworn I heard the owl-eyed man break into ghostly laughter.

We went upstairs, through period bedrooms swathed in rose and lavender silk and vivid with new flowers, through dressing-rooms and pool-rooms, and bathrooms, with sunken baths—intruding into one chamber where a dishevelled man in pajamas was doing liver exercises on the floor. It was Mr. Klipspringer, the "boarder." I had seen him wandering hungrily about the beach that morning. Finally we came to Gatsby's own apartment, a bedroom and a bath, and an Adam study, where we sat down and drank a glass of some Chartreuse he took from a cupboard in the wall.

He hadn't once ceased looking at Daisy, and I think he revalued everything in his house according to the measure of response it drew from her well-loved eyes. Sometimes, too, he stared around at his possessions in a dazed way, as though in her actual and astounding presence none of it was any longer real. Once he nearly toppled down a flight of stairs.

His bedroom was the simplest room of all—except where the dresser was garnished with a toilet set of pure dull gold. Daisy took the brush with delight, and smoothed her hair, whereupon Gatsby sat down and shaded his eyes and began to laugh.

"It's the funniest thing, old sport," he said hilariously. "I can't—when I try to—"

He had passed visibly through two states and was entering upon a third. After his embarrassment and his unreasoning joy he was consumed with wonder at her presence. He had been full of the idea so long, dreamed it right through to the end, waited with his teeth set, so to speak, at an inconceivable pitch of intensity. Now, in the reaction, he was running down like an overwound clock.

Recovering himself in a minute he opened for us two hulking patent cabinets which held his massed suits and dressing-gowns and ties, and his shirts, piled like bricks in stacks a dozen high.

"I've got a man in England who buys me clothes. He sends over a selection of things at the beginning of each season, spring and fall."

He took out a pile of shirts and began throwing them, one by one, before us, shirts of sheer linen and thick silk and fine flannel, which lost their folds as they fell and covered the table in many-colored disarray. While we admired he brought more and the soft rich heap

1960

mounted higher—shirts with stripes and scrolls and plaids in coral and apple-green and lavender and faint orange, with monograms of Indian blue. Suddenly, with a strained sound, Daisy bent her head into the shirts and began to cry stormily.

"They're such beautiful shirts," she sobbed, her voice muffled in the thick folds. "It makes me sad because I've never seen such—such beautiful shirts before."

F. Scott Fitzgerald
The Great Gatsby, 1925

After the Banquet has been called Yukio Mishima's most elegant novel, and it does indeed reveal the noted Japanese novelist's abiding concern with the subtlest nuances of social behavior. Characters are not so much described as they are defined—by their manners, their modes of speech, and their taste in clothing. In no case is this more true than with Mishima's heroine, Kazu, the independently wealthy wife of politician Yuken Noguchi. For example, she campaigns in "a kimono dyed with a pattern of white horsetails and dandelions on black slubbed crepe"—a design that suggests the character no, *or meadow, the first syllable in her husband's surname. The campaign concluded, Kazu and Noguchi dress to go to the polls.*

Kazu had thrown all her money and energies into the campaign. She had done all that human strength was capable of, and she had patiently endured every humiliation and hardship. Everyone knew that Kazu had fought well. Never before in her life had her passionate spirit been poured out so continuously and so effectively. Day after day her unique support had been her absurd conviction that once she put her mind to do something she would certainly bring it to fruition. This conviction of hers normally hovered vaguely in mid-air, but during the past few months it had been planted firmly on earth, and she could no longer live without it.

Kazu attentively examined the water lilies. The water seemed to be a symbol of the countless people who would go today to the polling places in each district. The blossoming water lilies were Noguchi himself. The water under the flowers soaked the reflections in its depths, and bubbles rose as it stirred round each tiny spike of the flower-holder. The water's only function, she thought, was to crave the favor of the lily blossoms and reflect them.

Just then a bird's shadow darted across the open bay window, and a withered leaf was flicked from a small branch reaching almost to the window. It glided sledlike through the air to drop into the basin. The water was hardly ruffled, but the shrunken yellow-brown leaf floated conspicuously on its surface. It looked ugly, like a curled-up insect.

If Kazu had not been practicing her incautious divination, she would have removed the withered leaf without giving it a second thought, but now its ominous appearance so upset her that she bitterly regretted her folly in having started this fortunetelling.

She dropped into an armchair and sat there a while, toying with a fan. A television set stood directly before her. The bluish viewing screen would soon no doubt be displaying the election returns as they came in, but now it was still a blank. The morning sunlight slanted across its surface.

Kazu took her morning bath after Noguchi, carefully made up her face, then changed to a formal kimono ordered some time previously for this occasion. After days of campaigning during which she had taken no trouble with her appearance—sometimes deliberately dressing badly—her holiday finery today braced her body. The kimono was a silvery gray gauzy silk dyed to represent a cormorant fishing scene. The cormorants were lacquer-black, and the torch flames blazed scarlet. The obi, of brocaded silk, had an embroidered design of a waning moon amid thin clouds, worked in silver thread on a pale blue background. A diamond sash clip graced her outfit.

Kazu realized that such an ornate costume was likely to annoy Noguchi, but she was determined to be dressed to her own satisfaction when she went to the polling place. In any case, now that the sweat and dust of the campaign were behind her, Kazu needed to assuage her feelings by indulging herself today, while things were still un-settled, in some luxury after her heart.

She went to the drawing room to help Noguchi with his dressing. The sight of him standing there filled Kazu's heart with joy. Noguchi was already dressed, and had himself chosen, from among the suits carefully pressed by Kazu's command, the new one he first wore on the day when he announced his intention of standing for office.

Noguchi, as usual, did not vouchsafe her even the flicker of a smile, but this thoughtfulness and his avoidance of any reference to her costume touched her deeply. In the car on the way to the polling place, they sat side-by-side in silence. Kazu looked out the window at the row of shops exposed to the merciless morning sunlight. Now that she had had such an unforgettable experience, she felt that it did not matter any more if they lost.

This, probably, was the moment of greatest intimacy between a husband and wife with such unyielding personalities. Kazu's euphoria was maintained intact until she followed her husband, through the popping flashbulbs and arc-lamps of the newspapers and newsreel cameramen, into the polling place in an elementary school, and cast her ballot in the box.

The counting of the ballots began the following day. Election fore-casts printed in the three major morning newspapers showed a re-markably even distribution of opinion. One political expert predicted the victory of Tobita, another foresaw victory for Noguchi, and a third, without mentioning which side would win, predicted that it

1965

would undoubtedly be a photo finish with only a nose-length between the two men. Kazu's state of frantic excitement had started that morning. A premonition of victory agitated her, and with it the conviction that if they didn't win the world would crumble to pieces. The counting of ballots began at eight in the morning, and at eleven the first bulletin was issued. Husband and wife sat before the television set in the living room. The first to report were the Santama region and the outlying metropolitan districts.

Kazu, unable to contain her palpitations, murmured as if intoning a magic spell, "It's Santama, Santama!" She suddenly recalled the strings of paper lanterns on the night of the Folk Song Festival, the blackness of the surrounding mountains when the lanterns were lit, and the enthusiastic applause echoing against the mountainsides. The sunburned faces of the farm wives, their little eyes filled with curiosity, and their friendly gold-toothed smiles all came back. . . . She dug her fingernails into the armrests of her chair. The suspense made her feel suddenly hot and cold by turns. Finally she could keep silent no longer.

"That's a lucky sign," she cried, "Santama will be first to report. That's one place we surely won."

Noguchi did not answer.

The news bulletin flashed on the television screen, and the voice of the announcer echoed as he read:

| Yuken Noguchi | 257,802 |
| Gen Tobita | 277,081 |

The color drained from Kazu's face, but her desperate resolve not to lose hope became like a sheet of iron wrapped around her heart.

YUKIO MISHIMA
After the Banquet, 1963

Although Sinclair Lewis should properly be remembered as the first American author to win the Nobel Prize for literature—in 1930—many thousands of readers know him as the creator of George F. Babbitt, the archetypal Average American, a mixture of blandness and boosterism, prejudice and pomposity, crassness and conservatism. Babbitt, a middle-aged, middle-class, middle-of-the-road realtor from Zenith, "the Zip City," is, like his carefully chosen wardrobe, "completely undistinguished."

Myra Babbitt—Mrs. George F. Babbitt—was definitely mature. She had creases from the corners of her mouth to the bottom of her chin, and her plump neck bagged. But the thing that marked her as having passed the line was that she no longer had reticences before her husband, and no longer worried about not having reticences. She was in a petticoat now, and corsets which bulged, and unaware of being seen in bulgy corsets. She had become so dully habituated to married life

COUTURE 71
for Davidow

1970

that in her full matronliness she was as sexless as an anemic nun. She was a good woman, a kind woman, a diligent woman, but no one, save perhaps Tinka her ten-year-old, was at all interested in her or entirely aware that she was alive.

After a rather thorough discussion of all the domestic and social aspects of towels she apologized to Babbit for his having an alcoholic headache; and he recovered enough to endure the search for a B.V.D. undershirt which had, he pointed out, malevolently been concealed among his clean pajamas.

He was fairly amiable in the conference on the brown suit.

"What do you think, Myra?" He pawed at the clothes hunched on a chair in their bedroom, while she moved about mysteriously adjusting and patting her petticoat and, to his jaundiced eye, never seeming to get on with her dressing. "How about it? Shall I wear the brown suit another day?"

"Well, it looks awfully nice on you."

"I know, but gosh, it needs pressing."

"That's so. Perhaps it does."

"It certainly could stand being pressed, all right."

"Yes, perhaps it wouldn't hurt it to be pressed."

"But gee, the coat doesn't need pressing. No sense in having the whole darn suit pressed, when the coat doesn't need it."

"That's so."

"But the pants certainly need it, all right. Look at them—look at those wrinkles—the pants certainly do need pressing."

"That's so. Oh, Georgie, why couldn't you wear the brown coat with the blue trousers we were wondering what we'd do with them?"

"Good Lord! Did you ever in all my life know me to wear the coat of one suit and the pants of another? What do you think I am? A busted bookkeeper?"

1975

"Well, why don't you put on the dark gray suit to-day, and stop in at the tailor and leave the brown trousers?"

"Well, they certainly need—Now where the devil is that gray suit? Oh, yes, here we are."

He was able to get through the other crises of dressing with comparative resoluteness and calm.

His first adornment was the sleeveless dimity B.V.D. undershirt, in which he resembled a small boy humorlessly wearing a cheesecloth tabard at a civic pageant. He never put on B.V.D.'s without thanking the God of Progress that he didn't wear tight, long, old-fashioned undergarments, like his father-in-law and partner, Henry Thompson. His second embellishment was combing and slicking back his hair. It gave him a tremendous forehead, arching up two inches beyond the former hair-line. But most wonder-working of all was the donning of his spectacles.

There is character in spectacles—the pretentious tortoise-shell, the meek pince-nez of the school teacher, the twisted silver-framed glasses of the old villager. Babbitt's spectacles had huge, circular, frameless lenses of the very best glass; the ear-pieces were thin bars of gold. In them he was the modern business man; one who gave orders to clerks and drove a car and played occasional golf and was scholarly in regard to Salesmanship. His head suddenly appeared not babyish but weighty, and you noted his heavy, blunt nose, his straight mouth and thick, long upper lip, his chin overfleshy but strong; with respect you beheld him put on the rest of his uniform as a Solid Citizen.

The gray suit was well cut, well made, and completely undistinguished. It was a standard suit. White piping on the V of the vest added a flavor of law and learning. His shoes were black laced boots, good boots, honest boots, standard boots, extraordinarily uninteresting boots. The only frivolity was in his purple knitted scarf. With considerable comment on the matter to Mrs. Babbitt (who, acrobatically fastening the back of her blouse to her skirt with a safety-pin, did not hear a word he said), he chose between the purple scarf and a tapestry effect with stringless brown harps among blown palms, and into it he thrust a snake-head pin with opal eyes.

A sensational event was changing from the brown suit to the gray the contents of his pockets. He was earnest about these objects. They were of eternal importance, like baseball or the Republican Party. They included a fountain pen and a silver pencil (always lacking a supply of new leads) which belonged in the righthand upper vest pocket. Without them he would have felt naked. On his watch-chain were a gold penknife, silver cigar-cutter, seven keys (the use of two of which he had forgotten), and incidentally a good watch. Depending from the chain was a large, yellowish elk's-tooth—proclamation of his membership in the Brotherly and Protective Order of Elks. Most significant of all was his loose-leaf pocket note-book, that modern and efficient note-book which contained the addresses of people whom he had forgotten, prudent memoranda of postal money-orders which had reached their destinations months ago, stamps which had lost their mucilage, clippings of verses by T. Cholmondeley Frink and of the newspaper editorials from which Babbitt got his opinions and his polysyllables, notes to be sure and do things which he did not intend to do, and one curious inscription—D.S.S.D. M.Y.P.D.F.

But he had no cigarette-case. No one had ever happened to give him one, so he hadn't the habit, and people who carried cigarette-cases he regarded as effeminate.

Last, he stuck in his lapel the Boosters' Club button. With the conciseness of great art the button displayed two words: "Boosters—Pep!" It made Babbitt feel loyal and important. It associated him with Good Fellows, with men who were nice and human, and important in business circles. It was his V.C., his Legion of Honor ribbon, his Phi Beta Kappa key.

With the subtleties of dressing ran other complex worries. "I feel kind of punk this morning," he said. "I think I had too much dinner last evening. You oughtn't to serve those heavy banana fritters."

"But you asked me to have some."

"I know, but—I tell you, when a fellow gets past forty he has to look after his digestion. There's a lot of fellows that don't take proper care of themselves. I tell you at forty a man's a fool or his doctor—I mean, his own doctor. Folks don't give enough attention to this matter of dieting. Now I think—Course a man ought to have a good meal after the day's work, but it would be a good thing for both of us if we took lighter lunches."

"But Georgie, here at home I always do have a light lunch."

"Mean to imply I make a hog of myself, eating down-town? Yes, sure! You'd have a swell time if you had to eat the truck that new steward hands out to us at the Athletic Club! But I certainly do feel out of sorts, this morning. Funny, got a pain down here on the left side—but no, that wouldn't be appendicitis, would it? Last night, when I was driving over to Verg Gunch's, I felt a pain in my stomach, too. Right here it was—kind of a sharp shooting pain. I—Where'd that dime go to? Why don't you serve more prunes at breakfast? Of course I eat an apple every evening—an apple a day keeps the doctor away—but still, you ought to have more prunes, and not all those fancy doodads."

"The last time I had prunes you didn't eat them."

"Well, I didn't feel like eating 'em, I suppose. Matter of fact, I think I did eat some of 'em. Anyway—I tell you it's mighty important to—I was saying to Verg Gunch, just last evening, most people don't take sufficient care of their diges—"

"Shall we have the Gunches for our dinner, next week,"

"Why sure; you bet."

"Now see here, George: I want you to put on your nice dinner-jacket that evening."

"Rats! The rest of 'em won't want to dress."

"Of course they will. You remember when you didn't dress for the Littlefields' supper-party, and all the rest did, and how embarrassed you were."

"Embarrassed, hell! I wasn't embarrassed. Everybody knows I can put on as expensive a Tux. as anybody else, and I should worry if I don't happen to have it on sometimes. All a darn nuisance, anyway. All right for a woman, that stays around the house all the time, but when a fellow's worked like the dickens all day, he doesn't want to go and hustle his head off getting into the soup-and-fish for a lot of folks that he's seen in just reg'lar clothes that same day."

"You know you enjoy being seen in one. The other evening you admitted you were glad I'd insisted on your dressing. You said you felt a lot better for it. And oh, Georgie, I do wish you wouldn't say 'Tux.' It's 'dinner-jacket.' "

"Rats, what's the odds,"

"Well, it's what all the nice folks say. Suppose Lucile McKelvey heard you calling it a 'Tux.' "

"Well, that's all right now! Lucile McKelvey can't pull anything on me! Her folks are common as mud, even if her husband and her dad are millionaires! I suppose you're trying to rub in *your* exalted social position! Well, let me tell you that your revered paternal ancestor, Henry T., doesn't even call it a 'Tux.'! He calls it a 'bobtail jacket for a ringtail monkey,' and you couldn't get him into one unless you chloroformed him!"

"Now don't be horrid, George."

"Well, I don't want to be horrid, but Lord! you're getting as fussy as Verona."

SINCLAIR LEWIS
Babbitt, 1922

Glossary

BABY DRESS *See robe à la creole.*

BLIAUT A long overtunic worn by both men and women from the eleventh to the late thirteenth century. The male version had full sleeves and was split to the waist so it could be worn over chain mail. The female version had a more closely fitted bodice and also featured full sleeves.

CALASH A collapsible bonnet designed to accommodate the fantastic hairstyles of the late 1700's.

CARMAGNOLE A short jacket with wide collar and lapels worn by French revolutionaries.

CHEMISE The basic undergarment worn by women, it was a straight, unshaped linen shift that could double as a nightgown. A variation of it was worn by men until the shirt was developed.

CHEMISE GOWN A long-sleeved, tubular dress, usually made up in a soft, clinging muslin, its shape defined by drawstrings at the neck and at the high waist.

CHITON The basic Ionic costume for women, it was similar to the peplos but of linen rather than wool and much more voluminous. Slits for the arms were left at the top, which was caught together at intervals along the upper arm by seaming or by tiny brooches or studs. It was tied at the waist with a narrow cord, the upper part pulled out over the cord to give a blouselike effect. Narrower versions were worn by men.

CHLAMYS In Ancient Greece, a short rectangular cloak of wool worn in place of the himation. It was worn for traveling or for military activity.

CLAVI A vertical border used by the Etruscans to decorate their tunics. It was adopted by the Romans, who strictly regulated its width and color according to social standing.

CODPIECE Although usually cut from the same material as the trunk hose or breeches, this was a separate piece of cloth designed to cover the opening of the hose. It was laced to the hose and doublet with points, and by the sixteenth century was heavily boned and padded.

COTEHARDIE A tunic worn by both sexes from the twelfth through the fourteenth century. In the early Renaissance it was modified into a man's short jacket with long, closefitting sleeves buttoned from elbow to wrist. Cut very tightly to the body, it reached to the upper thigh and usually buttoned down the front.

CYCLAS A sleeveless overtunic worn during ancient and medieval times.

DALMATIC A long garment with straight or flaring sleeves that originated in Dalmatia and was popular during the third century. It was retained in the Middle Ages as court costume and still survives in religious regalia.

DOUBLET The male upper garment that had evolved from the pourpoint by the end of the 1400's. It fell to the waist and had a low neckline and was standard male attire through the sixteenth and seventeenth centuries.

EXOMIS The basic working-class garment of ancient Greece, it consisted of a plain strip of cloth fastened on the left shoulder, leaving the right arm free. It was usually belted at the waist and fell to about mid-thigh.

FARTHINGALE A framework of graduated cane or metal hoops worn around the hips to support the skirt in the 1500's. Both cone-shaped and wheel-shaped varieties were popular.

FLEA COAT A shaggy Renaissance lounging robe, often of wolfskin, whose purpose was to attract fleas. By the sixteenth century, it had become a mere flea fur, the hide of a small animal elegantly mounted in gold and gems and carried in the hand or draped around the arm like a stole.

FRENCH HOOD A neatly rounded little cap set far back on the head. It was introduced to the English court by Anne Boleyn.

GARDE-INFANTE A mid-seventeenth-century elliptical hooped petticoat, very narrow from front to back but which extended on either side of the waist to a width greater than the reach of the arms. It was worn by women of the Spanish royal family and the court.

GAULLE *See robe à la creole.*

HAIK Worn by Egyptian royalty, this was a large, rectangular piece of cloth that was knotted and draped around the body in such a manner that the wearer appeared to have on three garments—a short kilt, a tunic, and a long cloak. It survives in a modified form in traditional Arabic costume.

HIMATION A long woolen robe worn by both sexes in ancient Greece. It was draped around the body and tucked in at the waist.

HOUPPELANDE A loose outer tunic, belted high at the waist and with extremely full, flaring sleeves, worn by both men and women in the fourteenth and fifteenth centuries.

JUSTAUCORPS A term in France in the seventeenth and eighteenth centuries to refer to a man's jacket. It had no collar and was worn with a sleeveless vest, and closefitting knee-length breeches.

KALASIRIS A straight sheath dress worn by Egyptian women and made from a rectangular piece of linen sewn up the side. The dress was supported by shoulder straps; sometimes these were broad and covered the breasts; sometimes the breasts were left bare. In the New Kingdom, it became more elaborate, being made of almost transparent linen finely pleated and wraped around the body in various ways. Sometimes it was cut with sleeves, sometimes merely draped and tied to give a sleeved effect.

KAUNAKES A fabric from the Near East in the third millennium B.C. that was made by threading tufts of wool or loosely rolled yarn through a coarsely woven panel cloth; tufts were brushed or combed toward the hem of the finished garment.

NEGLIGE A LA PATRIOTE A white dress worn under a blue redingote with a red collar during the time of the French Revolution.

PALLA The Roman version of the Greek himation.

PANIERS Elliptical hoops worn in the eighteenth century that concentrated fullness at the sides of a dress rather than at the front and rear.

PEPLOS A long robe worn by Doric women, it reached from shoulder to ankle with a generous overfold at the top falling to the waist. At the shoulders it was caught and held by two large pins. It could be belted at the waist, sewn up the side, or, in Spartan fashion, left open on the right side.

PETTICOAT BREECHES Mid-seventeenth-century open-legged trousers so full they looked like skirts. They reached to the knee or even mid-calf and were worn with a short matching doublet.

POLONAISE A short, late-eighteenth-century gown reaching well above the ankle and worn over modest hoops. The overskirt, heavily flounced, was hiked up by drawstrings to form three rounded, puffed swags of varying lengths, one at either side and one in the rear.

POURPOINT A man's upper garment similar to the cotehardie. It was derived from the padded military jacket of the fourteenth century. In the fifteenth century, the term was an alternate name for the doublet.

RHINEGRAVES *See Petticoat breeches.*

ROBE A L'ANGLAISE A gown of the late eighteenth century boned closely to the waist and worn

183

without paniers or hoops. The skirt was gathered at the hips and had a short train. A *cul de Paris* held out the fullness at the rear.

ROBE A LA CREOLE   An extremely simple dress, scarcely more than a chemise, caught in at the waist with a wide sash. Generally of delicate white muslin or gauze, it was worn without hoops over light petticoats, with or without stays.

ROBE A LA FRANCAISE   A dress derived from the earlier sack gown with a pleated back train and an overskirt split over a petticoat. It was worn over elliptical hoops or paniers, which concentrated the fullness at the sides only, leaving both the front and rear of the gown quite flat. An extremely popular style, it was much favored by Mme de Pompadour and was worn well into the 1770's.

RUFF   A costume accessory worn by both men and women in the late sixteenth and throughout the seventeenth centuries. It consisted of a long strip of fine linen or lace, heavily starched and gathered on the inner edge to a neckband. At their widest, cartwheel or millstone ruffs had a radius of over eighteen inches.

SACK GOWN   A loose, early eighteenth-century dress featuring double box pleats set in on a straight-back neckline to fall unbelted to the ground in a train. In front, the pleats converged to a point low on the waistline with the opening either sewn or caught together with bows. It could also be worn open in front to show the petticoat. Popularly known as the Watteau gown.

SANS-CULOTTES   Wide, floppy trousers, long the standard costume of the French workingman. Literally the term means "no knee breeches," garments worn by men of the middle and upper classes. The term applied to French revolutionaries as well as to their trousers.

SHIRTWAIST   A woman's tailored blouse first popular in the late nineteenth century.

SLASHING   The Renaissance practice of cutting openings in the outer costume and pulling the inner garments or the lining out through the slits.

SPANISH BODY   A heavy corset worn by women in the mid-1500's.

SPENCER   A short, fitted high-necked jacket originally worn by women with the chemise dress and in vogue until 1830. Later, the style was adopted by the military for an officer's mess jacket.

STOLA   The basic garment worn by Roman women, it was derived from and almost identical to the Ionic chiton.

TEBENNA   The distinctive Etruscan cloak, semicircular in shape, that became the prototype for the Roman toga.

TOGA   The national costume of ancient Rome, this garment was usually of wool and went through several changes in cut and draping that paralled the growth of Rome itself. During the Republic, the toga was a simple, all-purpose wrap whose prototype was the Etruscan tebenna. As the republic expanded into an empire, the toga likewise expanded until it measured twenty feet in length and the manner in which it was draped became intricate and complex. The garment was to become so cumbersome that it was gradually abandoned.

TOGA CANDIDA   The garment, bleached a dazzling white, that was worn by Roman candidates for office.

TOGA PICTA   A rich purple garment, heavily embroidered with gold, that was awarded to victorious Roman generals and, later on, emperors and consuls.

TOGA PRAETEXTA   The garment that freeborn sons of Roman citizens started out life in. It was white with a band of scarlet or purple along the straight edge.

TOGA PULLA   A black or dark-colored garment worn by Roman mourners.

TOGA TRABEA   A short garment with a scarlet stripe and a purple hem that was worn by Roman augurs and certain priests.

TOGA VIRILIS   The plain garment of natural, unbleached wool that a Roman male put on when, at about the age of sixteen, he reached manhood.

WAISTCOAT   *See justaucorps.*

WATTEAU GOWN   *See sack gown.*

Acknowledgments

The Author wishes to thank the library staff of the Fashion Institute of Technology and the Shirley Goodman Design Resource Center for assisting her in her research for this book.

Picture Credits

The Editors would like to thank Russell Ash in London, Barbara Nagelsmith in Paris, and Susan Stover in New York for their invaluable assistance.

The following abbreviations are used:

> BNP—Bibliothèque Nationale, Paris
> G—Giraudon, Paris
> MMA—Metropolitan Museum of Art
> NGA—National Gallery of Art, Washington
> NYPL—New York Public Library
> S—Scala

HALF TITLE Symbol by Jay J. Smith Studio TITLE PAGE Hui Tsung, *Ladies Preparing Newly Woven Silk*, Sung Dynasty, 12th century. Museum of Fine Arts, Boston.

CHAPTER 1 **6** Michelangelo, *Expulsion from the Garden of Eden*. Sistine Chapel (S) **8** Venus of Lespugne. St. Germain-en-Laye (G) **9** top, Rendering of the Sorcerer from the cave of Les Trois Frères, Musée de l'Homme; bottom, Bernardino de Sahagun, *Historia de las Cosas* . . . , Codex Fiorentino, Biblioteca Laurenziana, Florence. **10** top, Antonio Moro, *Queen Mary*, 1554, Isabella Stewart Gardner Museum; bottom, Jacques-Louis David, *Young Woman in White*. NGA Chester Dale Collection, 1962. **11** J.A.D. Ingres, *Madame Moitessier*, NGA, Kress Collection, 1946. **13** top, Japanese helmet and mask, 16th-18th centuries, MMA, gift of Bashford Dean, 1914; bottom Reconstruction of the Mayan Bonampak murals, Museo Nacional de Antropología, Mexico City. **14** Museum of African Art, Eliot Elisofon Archives. **15** Anna Held, 1900. Library of Congress.

CHAPTER 2 **16** Queen Merit Amon, Deir el Bahari, 18th Dynasty. Egyptian Museum, Cairo. **18** Sumerian statue of Ibikil, Ishtar Temple, Mari. Louvre. **19** Gudea of Lagash, Mesopotamia, *ca.* 2150 B.C. MMA, Harris Brisbane Dick Fund, 1959. **20** Fresco from the Tomb of Queen Nefertari, Luxor. (Borromeo) **21** Model of a weaving shop, Middle Kingdom. MMA anon. gift, 1930. **22** Relief from Tomb of Ramose, Thebes. (George Holton) **22–23** Fresco of Tutankhamen, Valley of the Kings. (Fiore) **23** Methethy and his sons, 6th Dynasty. William Rockhill Nelson Gallery, Kansas City. **24** left, Pectoral and necklace, 18th Dynasty. Louvre (S); right, Tutankhamen's corselet, 18th Dynasty. Egyptian Museum, Cairo (John Ross) **26** Tutankhamen's treasure. Egyptian Museum, Cairo (Borromeo) **27** Fresco of Semite envoys, Tomb of Sebekhotep, 1420 B.C. British Museum (Holford) **28** Assyrian reliefs of king and warrior. (Fiore) **29** Relief of Ashurbanipal, Nineveh, 7th century B.C. British Museum (Holford) **30–31** Sarcophagus from Hagia Triada, Minoan Heraklion Museum (S) **32** Statue of the snake goddess from Temple at Knossos, Minoan. Heraklion Museum (S) **30** Gold earrings, Mycenaean, Acropolis Museum.

CHAPTER 3 **34** Zeus with attendants, Amphora, 6th century B.C. British Museum (Holford) **36** top, Caryatids on the Erechtheum, Acropolis (Archivio B); bottom, Relief of the Three Charities. Museo Chiaramonti, Vatican (S) **37** Archaic kore, *ca.* 500 B.C. Acropolis Museum. **38** Bronze charioteer, 475 B.C. Delphi Mu-

seum. **39** Frieze of Archers of the Royal Guard, Susa, 4th century B.C. Louvre (S)
40–41 Relief of warriors, Persepolis. (Fiore) **42–43** Dancers from the Tomb of
Triclionio, Tarquinia. (S) **44** left, Relief from the Arch of Marcus Aurelius,
Museo Capitolino; right, Statue of Tiberius. Louvre (G) **45** Statue of Titus.
Museo Nazionale Naples. **46–47** Fresco from the Villa dei Misteri, Pompeii (S)
49 left, Head of a Roman woman. Museo Capitolino; right, Relief from a sepulcher,
200 A.D. Landesmuseum, Trier.

CHAPTER 4 **50** Otto II, *Le Maitre de Registrum Gregori, ca. 985.* Musée Condé,
Chantilly. **53** Gundestrup Cauldron. National Museum, Copenhagen. **54** Mosaic
of Empress Theodora, San Vitale, Ravenna. (Pucciarelli) **55** *Homilies of St. John
Chrysostom,* 11th century. BNP, Paris, Ms. Coislin 79 fol 2v. **56–57** *La Vie de St.
Denys,* 13th century. BNP Nouv. Acquis. 1098, fol 50. **58** Charlemagne's dalmatic.
Treasury, St. Peter's, Vatican (S) **60** *Moralia in Job,* 12th century. Bibliothèque
Municipale, Dijon Ms. 168 fol 4v. **61** Royal Portal, Chartres. Archives Photo-
graphiques **62–63** The Bayeux Tapestry. Bayeux Museum (S) **64** Sketchbook of
Villard de Honnecourt, 1225. BNP Ms. Fr. 19093 fol 23v. **65** left, Knight from
Rheims Cathedral, Archives Photographique; right, English knight, 1250. Pierpont
Morgan Library M. 638 fol 28.

CHAPTER 5 **66** Jean Clouet, *François I.* Louvre (G) **48** *Scenes from the Life of
St. Mark,* 14th century. Catedral de Manresa (MAS) **69** left, Luca della Robbia,
symbol of the Florentine wool guild, Museo dell 'Opera del Duomo, Florence (S);
right, The textile market, Bologna, 1470 Museo Civico, Bologna (S) **70** A. Loren-
zetti, *Buon Governo in Citta.* Palazzo Publico, Siena (S) **71** *Grandes Heures du
Duc de Berry.* 15th century. BNP Ms. Lat. 18014 fol 228v. **72–73** *Livre des Tour-
nois de Roi Rene,* 1460. BNP Ms. Fr. 2695 fols. 67–68. **74** Pisanello, *Woman in
Court Costume.* Musée Condé, Chantilly (G) **74–75** Maestro del Cassone Adimari,
Marriage of Boccaccio Adimari, 15th century. Accademia, Florence (S) **76** Hunt
at the court of Philip the Good, 15th century. Versailles (G) **77** Tapestry, Arras,
ca. 1435. MMA, Rogers Fund, 1909. **79** left, *Portrait of a Lady,* Franco-Flemish,
15th century; right, Rogier van der Weyden, *Portrait of a Lady,* 15th century.
Both: NGA, Mellon Collection, 1937. **80** left, Lucas Cranach the Elder, *Duke
Henry the Pious,* 1514. Pinakothek, Dresden; right, Titian, *Alessandro Alberti.*
NGA, Kress Collection, 1952. **82** top, Hans Holbein, *Anne Boleyn,* Weston Park/
Courtauld Institute; center, Henry VIII's armor, Tower of London; bottom, Hans
Holbein, *Anne of Cleves.* Louvre. **83** Hans Holbein, *Jane Seymour.* Kunsthistor-
isches Museum, Vienna. **84–85** Robert Peake. *A Procession of Queen Elizabeth,*
1597. Simon Wingfield, M.P. **86** Nicholas Hilliard, *Miniature of a Young Man,*
1588. Victoria and Albert Museum.

CHAPTER 6 **88** Peter Paul Rubens, *The Artist and His First Wife, Isabella Brandt,*
1610. Pinakothek, Munich. **90–91** *Ball of the Court of Henry III,* 16th century.
Louvre (G) **93** Anton Van Dyck, *Gaston de France, Duc d'Orléans.* Musée
Condé Chantilly. **94–95** Italian undergarments, 16th century. MMA, Rogers
Fund, 1910 **97** Hyacinthe Rigaud, *Louis XIV.* Louvre. **98–99** Antoine Trouvain,
Apartemens, 1695. Minneapolis Institute of Arts, Minnich Collection. **99** Louise
de la Vallière. BNP **100–101** Ball at the court of Louis XIV, 18th century.
Musée de Arts Décoratifs, Paris. **102** Man's suit, French, 1725. MMA Rogers
Fund, 1911. **104** Antoine Watteau, detail from *The Gersaint Shop.* Charlotten-
burg, Berlin (G) **105** Maurice Quentin de la Tour, *Mme de Pompadour.*
Louvre. **106** American Fashion dolls, *ca.* 1790. MMA Bequest of Maria James,
1911. **107** François Boucher, *Le Dejeuner.* Louvre. **108** Jean Moreau, *Rendez-
vous pour Marly,* 1780. Minneapolis Institute of Arts, Minnich Collection. **109**
top, Marie Antoinette. BNP; bottom, Antoine Raspal, *Atelier de Couture à Arles.*
Musée Realtu, Arles (AME) **111** Fashion plates from *Galerie de Modes et
Costumes. Français* . . . 1817–87. NYPL. **112** M. Darly, *Tight Lacing,* 1776.
MMA, Dick Fund, 1941.

CHAPTER 7 **114** Pierre Paul Prud'hon, *Rutger Jan Schimmelpenninck and His Family*. 1901. Rijksmuseum, Amsterdam. **117** *Le Bon Genre*, plate 27. MMA, Dick Fund, 1938. **118–19** J.L. David, *Coronation of Napoleon*, 1804. Louvre. **120** Fashion plates from *Petit Courrier des Dames*, 1827–33. NYPL. **121** George Cruikshank, *Life in London*, 1821. NYPL. **122–23** R. Sharples, *Cloakroom at an Assembly Rooms Ball*, 1817. City Art Gallery, Bristol. **124** T. Phillips, *Lord Byron*. National Portrait Gallery, London. **125** *La Belle Assemblie*, 1828. NYPL. **126** Thomas McLean, *The Bustle*. NYPL. **126–27** top, Thomas McLean, . . . *Winding up the Ladies*. NYPL; bottom, Robert Cruikshank, *Monstrosities of 1827*. NYPL. **128** BNP. **129** *Le Monde Elegant, 1860*. NYPL. **130** top, Corsets, Museum of the City of New York; bottom, Honore Daumier, *Croquis d'Hiver* . . . MMA, Rogers Fund 1922. **131** E. Guerard, *Les Tuileries*, 1856. Musée Carnavelet (G) **132** J. Worth evening dress, 1869. MMA, Rhinelander, 1946. **133** left, *Frank Leslie's Lady's Magazine*, 1870's. NYPL; right, *Journal des Demoiselles*, 1877. NYPL.

CHAPTER 8 **134** Irving Wiles, *Miss Julia Marlowe*, 1901. National Portrait Gallery, Washington. **136** Sears Roebuck Catalog, 1897. **139** left, Charles Dana Gibson, *The Gibson Book*. NYPL; right, NYPL. **140** Library of Congress. **143** Library of Congress. **145** *Gazette de Bon Ton*, 1920. NYPL. **146** & **147** Courtesy Dior. **147** Courtesy Chanel. **148–49** Guy Marineau **149** Sal Traina. Both: Courtesy WWD. **150** top left, Lester Sloan; center, Tony Rollo; others: Bernard Gotfryd. All: Newsweek. **151** top left, Robert McElroy; bottom right, Lester Sloan. Both: Newsweek. Others: Courtesy WWD.

IN A LITERARY FASHION **152–80** A selection of *Vogue* covers from 1900 to 1975. Courtesy Condé Nast (Bernard Gotfryd).

Selected Bibliography

Arnold, Janet. *A Handbook of Costume*. New York: Macmillan, 1973.

Black, J. Anderson and Garland, Madge. *A History of Fashion*. New York: Morrow, 1975.

Boucher, François. *20,000 Years of Fashion*. New York: Abrams, 1966.

Bradshaw, Angela. *World Costumes*. London: Black, 1952.

Broby-Johansen, R. *Body and Clothes*. New York: Reinhold, 1968.

Bruhn, Wolfgang. *A Pictorial History of Costume*. New York: Praeger, 1955.

Cunnington, C. Willett and Phillis. *The History of Underclothes*. London: Michael Joseph, 1951.

Davenport, Millia. *The Book of Costume*. New York: Crown, 1948.

Ewing, Elizabeth. *History of 20th Century Fashions*. New York: Scribners, 1974.

Garland, Madge. *The Changing Form of Fashion*. New York: Praeger, 1970.

Gorsline, Douglas. *What People Wore*. New York: Viking, 1952.

Harris, Christie and Johnston, Moira. *Figleafing Through History: The Dynamics of Dress*. New York: Atheneum, 1972.

Horn, M.J. *The Second Skin*. New York: Houghton Mifflin, 1968.

Kidwell, Claudia B. and Christman, Margaret C., *Suiting Everyone: The Democratization of Clothing in America*. Washington, D.C.: Smithsonian Inst. Press, 1975.

Köhler, Carl. *A History of Costume*. New York: Dover, 1963.

Kybalová, Ludmila. *Pictorial Encyclopedia of Fashion*. New York: Crown, 1968.

Laver, James. *Costume Through the Ages*. New York: Simon and Schuster, 1964.

——. *Modesty in Dress*. New York: Houghton Mifflin, 1969.

——. *The Concise History of Costume and Fashion*. New York: Scribners, 1974.

Payne, Blanche. *History of Costume*. New York: Harper and Row, 1965.

Rudofsky, Bernard. *The Unfashionable Human Body*. New York: Doubleday, 1971.

Squire, Geoffrey. *Dress and Society, 1560–1970*. New York: Viking, 1974.

Waugh, Nora. *Corsets and Crinolines*. New York: Theatre Arts Book, 1970.

Wilcox, R. Turner. *The Mode in Costume*. New York: Scribners, 1958.

Index